D1175866

JOSEF PIEPER AND *HEINZ RASKOP*

WHAT CATHOLICS BELIEVE

INTRODUCTION BY *Gerald B. Phelan*

TRANSLATION BY *Christopher Huntington*

PANTHEON

333 Sixth Avenue, New York 14, N. Y.

German title CHRISTENFIBEL
published by T. P. Bachem, Cologne

NIHIL OBSTAT:

THOMAS W. SMIDDY, S.T.L.
CENSOR LIBRORUM

IMPRIMATUR:

✠ THOMAS EDMUNDUS MOLLOY, S.T.D.
ARCHIEPISCOPUS-EPISCOPUS BROOKLYNIENSIS

Brooklyni, die VIII Iunii 1951.

Manufactured in the United States of America

CONTENTS

TRANSLATOR'S NOTE

In all but a few instances, quotations from the Old and New Testaments are from the translation by Ronald Knox. The other versions used were the Challoner-Rheims-Douay version, and its revision by the Confraternity of Christian Doctrine. In one instance (Wisdom 12:18, page 46), the translation is directly from the Vulgate, in agreement with the German.

With one exception on page 63, all quotations from the Missal are from the Knox-O'Connell edition of *The Missal in Latin and English, being the text of the Missale Romanum with English rubrics and a new translation,* New York (Sheed and Ward) 1949. Grateful acknowledgment is made to Sheed and Ward for their permission to use these translations.

I am greatly indebted to the Reverend Walter Farrell, O.P., for his careful reading of the translation, and for many valuable suggestions.

C. H.

INTRODUCTION

This little book on What Catholics Believe *offers a plain and simple statement of what every Catholic means deep down in his heart, when he says in making his Act of Faith, "Oh my God! I firmly believe all the sacred truths which the Holy Catholic Church believes and teaches because THOU has revealed them, Who canst neither deceive nor be deceived."*

This is not an argumentative book, not a work of controversy, nor even, strictly speaking, a "theological" study. It is rather a prolonged profession of Faith, fitted with the spiritually moving quality of the Athanasian or the Nicene Creed and the simple directness of the Sermon on the Mount. In a world torn by strife and conflict, where so many souls are groping for light and clamoring for God—from Whom the cruel teachings and traditions of secularist naturalism have cut them off—it is heartening to hear the age-old voice of Christian faith raised to proclaim, in all humility, the dogmatic and moral truths that have shaped and built the civilization for which thousands are now being called upon to shed their blood in war, and which uncounted multitudes the world over struggle valiantly, though often obscurely, to maintain against the inhumanity of communistic thought and the brutality of conduct it engenders.

The authors make no attempt to stir the emotions or to appeal to sentiment. Yet in their simple exposition of Catholic belief they have written a deeply moving book. They merely say, in effect: "This is what a Catholic means when he recites the Apostles' Creed; *this is what Catholics pray for when they say the* Our Father; *this is how Catholics believe God, in giving us the* Ten Commandments *and the* New Commandment *of which Christ spoke (John 13,34), requires us to live; this is how the Catholic Church fulfills her divine commission to teach all men and make of them disciples of Christ; this is what Catholics believe regarding the destiny of men in this life and beyond the grave." Nevertheless, the very calmness and unimpassioned simplicity of their statement of these profound Christian teachings communicates a soul-stirring experience. Like the reading of St. Augustine* On The Trinity, *St. Bernard* On The Love of God *or St. Bonaventure on* The Journey of the Soul to God, *this book leaves one with a feeling of deep humility arising from the thought that God, in His infinite wisdom, goodness and mercy, has given* me *that precious gift of Faith—that knowledge, conviction, and mysterious half-understanding of the most sublime truths—which so many others more worthy, it would seem, than* I, *have not received. To be so blessed by God prompts the soul to deepest and most humble gratitude, and arouses fervent zeal and earnest prayer to share with others—with all men—the gift we have, all undeservably, been given.*

Catholics are proud of *their faith, in the sense that they love and reverence all that God has taught and that they never cease to marvel at the wonders of His providence and the wisdom of His ways; but they are not proud* in *their faith, in the sense that they feel themselves superior to those who do not share their beliefs. On the contrary, they are constantly aware how unworthy they are of God's great condescension in revealing Himself as He has done to His ungrateful creatures; and they yearn and long and pray that all men's minds and hearts may be brought into the willing captivity of the loving Master whose yoke is so sweet and whose burden so light. The Church is not, for them, a dictator but a Mother. She is the Spouse of Christ, dispensing truth and grace and love and salvation to all men in His name and by His authority. What she teaches is not an arbitrary creed, but absolute truth.*

I not only BELIEVE, *but it is* true *that God, from all eternity, is a Triune God, One in Nature, Three in Person, Father, Son and Holy Ghost; it is* true *that Almighty God made the world, the angels and men; it is* true *that all men are children of Adam; it is* true *that our first parent "brought death into this world and all its woes" by his sin against God; it is* true *that Adam's sin deprived all his descendents (i.e., all men) of God's grace and friendship; it is* true *that Jesus Christ redeemed man from the slavery of sin, incurred by Adam's rebellion, and opened to him the way of salvation and the Gates of Heaven; it is* true *that the Holy, Roman, Catholic and Apostolic Church is the Mystical Body of Jesus Christ, the Incarnate Word of God; it is* true *that the Pope is the Vicar of Christ on earth; it is* true *that "the Gates of Hell" shall never prevail against that Kingdom of God.*

All this is not a matter of wishful thinking. Faith is not an affair of emotion; it is "reasonable homage," as St. Paul calls it. The truths of faith are true, *and reason bows to truth. These things are not true because I believe them; I believe them because they are true; and I wish, from the depths of my soul, that* all *my fellow men could see and know and love those truths as clearly, as staunchly, as humbly as God as given me to see and know and love them.*

Faith, however strong and unshakable, never makes anything to be true. Truth may give faith. Faith cannot give truth. What Catholics believe is not what they would like to be true but the truth—the whole truth and all *the truths—that God has so graciously, so mercifully and so lovingly taught us through his prophets of old, through His*

Only Begotten Son made Man, and through His Church, with Whom He abides all days, until the consummation of the world.

But, "Faith without good works is dead." A Catholic (i.e., one who believes all *the truths that God has taught) cannot escape, except by sinful evasion, the obligation to live in accordance with his beliefs. It was Chesterton—if my memory serves me—who first said that if one does not live as one thinks, it will not be long before one begins to think as one lives. Faith can be weakened, and even lost, if practice belies conviction.*

What Catholics believe implies and imposes an obligation to "live as one thinks." One cannot divorce faith from life without doing violence to both. And it is for this reason that the second half of the book, in which the authors deal with the life *of the Catholic, is as important as the first half, in which they state the* faith *or* beliefs *of Catholics. My only regret is that this second section was not expanded beyond its present dimensions. I am sure that the authors have much to say on this subject which for various reasons they have had to omit from this wonderful little title.*

Josef Pieper, the co-author of this simply beautiful and beautifully simple book, is not as well-known in this country as he is in his native Germany. For years his powerful influence has been felt in University circles in his homeland not only among philosophers and scholars but also among the great numbers of students who crowd his courses and flock to hear him wherever he may be lecturing. Dr. Pieper is probably the most outstanding Catholic lay apostle of Christian learning and culture in Germany today. His writings—with but one exception[1]*—have not yet ap-*

[1] *The Human Wisdom of St. Thomas.* Sheed and Ward, New York, 1948.

peared in English translation. The present little book will be only the second of his works to be published in English. A third book, Leisure the Basis of Culture, *with an introduction by T. S. Eliot, will appear shortly, published also by Pantheon Books, New York.*

All who met and conversed with Dr. Pieper, or followed his lectures during his recent sojourn in America,[2] *were aware that they had come to know a great and good Catholic, a true scholar, a man dedicated to the service of truth —or rather of Truth—and one admirably equipped to perform that service. I trust that his little book,* What Catholics Believe, *will be widely read in America.*

The Mediaeval Institute
University of Notre Dame
May 28, 1951.

GERALD B. PHELAN

[2] While he was a guest lecturer in the Departments of Political Science and Philosophy at the University of Notre Dame under the auspices of the Committee on International Affairs (1949–1950).

What Catholics Believe

CREATOR, beyond any words of ours to describe!

In the fullness of Your wisdom You have established the three celestial hierarchies of angels and set them in wonderfully ordered array over Your resplendent heaven. Most gloriously You have disposed all parts of the whole universe. You are the true source of light and wisdom, You are their first and final cause.

Pour out now, I beg You, a ray of Your clear light upon my murky understanding, and take from me my doubly dark inheritance of sin and ignorance. You who inspire the speech of little children, guide and teach my tongue now, and let the grace of Your blessing flow upon my lips. Grant me a sharp discernment, a strong memory, a methodical approach to study, a willing and able docility; let me be precise in interpretation and felicitous in choice of words.

Instruct my beginning, direct my progress, and bring my work to its proper finish: You, who are true God and true Man, living and reigning forever!

THOMAS AQUINAS

FAITH AND LIFE

The two distinguishing marks of a Christian are his faith or belief and his life, and these two things belong together. Just as knowledge and competent action go hand in hand, so do faith and life. Christian life requires Christian faith as its foundation; and Christian faith bears its full fruit in Christian life. Christian life without Christian belief is impossible; Christian belief without Christian life is unfruitful.

We must admit that something resembling a Christian life seems to be possible today without Christian belief. Some people appear to be able to order their lives in a Christian way whether they have any living faith in Christ or not. Actually, however, this phenomenon—a merely exterior Christian order—is nothing but the use of an inheritance by people who no longer truly possess it. Our forebears truly possessed it. With it they gave form to their life, order to their public weal, and character to their customs. The danger now is that we shall use up this inheritance altogether, unless in us belief once more comes to life.

That is why being a Christian here and now in our own age and in our own country means regaining the Christian faith, reviving it in us from its source, making it our own again through the grace of God. "It is faith," says St. Paul (Romans 1:17), "that brings life to the just man."

In what follows we shall therefore deal with two things: the belief or faith of the Christian, and his life.

THE FAITH OF THE CHRISTIAN

Faith, an Encounter with God

Christian faith is no mere matter of inner thoughts and feelings. It is an encounter with the reality of the Blessed Trinity. God, three persons in one nature (the Triune God), has been revealed to man by Jesus Christ, and the Christian faith is man's response to this revelation. So the first thing to be said about Christian faith is that in it the Christian touches upon a new reality which would otherwise remain unknown and closed to him.

The second thing is that we cannot make this response to the revelation of Jesus Christ of our own power. Of our own power we cannot perceive this new reality at all, let alone grasp it. To be sure, by our natural powers of knowing we can touch the surface, for it is within the scope of natural reason to know that God exists. But by nothing short of faith can a man in this life see the divine life in its fullness; and even with faith he sees it only as the reflection in a mirror and without ever fully comprehending God. Thus by Christian faith we mean not only the revealed reality of the Blessed Trinity but also the new power which man must be given to see it.

These are the reasons for calling Christian belief *supernatural*: faith is called supernatural because such belief exceeds our natural powers. Faith exceeds the nature of man, exceeding even the natural powers of his spirit. But Sacred Scripture (Luke 11:13) tells us that God our Father is "ready to give, from heaven, his Holy Spirit to those who ask him," and from this we know that the supernatural world visible through faith is closed to no man of good will.

For faith necessarily includes the assent of the intellect to truths that are not clear, and so an assent that has its basis in the free will. Supernatural gift that it is, it becomes our full personal possession only when we accept it voluntarily. We are free. The way lies open to us to say, "My natural eyes and ears and my natural reason are quite enough for me; any reality I cannot perceive with them is of little consequence as far as I am concerned." But whoever talks like this is rejecting in sheer wrongheadedness things of vital importance to him, including even the fulfillment of his own life. For our true and last destiny is eternal life, and only by faith do we learn of eternal life and the means to attain it. The attainment calls for putting our God-given powers to utmost possible use in this life before the restlessness of our whole being finally reaches in eternal life the equilibrium, tranquillity, and completion which it seeks. We know of this now because faith, as St. Paul says (Hebrews 11:1), "is that which gives substance to our hopes."

Our Profession of Faith, the Creed

You cannot profess belief in an incontestable fact which no one denies—in the fact, for instance, that the sun rises in the east. You can profess belief only in things which may be contested and denied.

Because the Christian faith may be contested and denied, it calls first and foremost for a profession of belief on the part of the Christian. The reason, however, that the Christian faith may be contested and denied is not that its content is dubious, but that the reality grasped by faith is concealed from our natural powers. It discloses itself only to him who with the help of divine grace wills to see it. The Christian faith may be denied because it requires the assent of the intellect that has its basis in the free will.

For this reason, the articles which establish the content of our faith are not a system of theoretical teachings. They are what they are called, "The Creed," which means "a confession of faith," an expression derived from the Latin *credo,* I believe.

The Sign of the Cross

There is one basic phrase which sums up in a few words, as it were in a blueprint, the whole Christian Creed, stressing our redemption through the sacrifice of Christ on the Cross. This is the phrase a Christian utters when he makes the sign of the Cross: "In the name of the Father and of the Son and of the Holy Ghost." In these words we give expression to the deepest and most basic mysteries of our faith—the mystery of our redemption through the sacrifice of Jesus Christ, and the mystery of the Most Holy Trinity.

All twelve clauses of the Creed are concerned with the activity of the Most Holy Trinity. The first article of faith speaks of God the Father and His work of creation. The next six speak of the Son and His work of redemption. The last five speak of the Holy Spirit (or Holy Ghost) and His work of sanctification.

THE CREED

I BELIEVE in God,
the Father almighty,
Creator of heaven and earth.

And in Jesus Christ
His only Son our Lord;
who was conceived by the Holy Ghost,
born of the Virgin Mary,
suffered under Pontius Pilate,
was crucified, died, and was buried;
He descended into hell;
the third day He rose again from the dead;
He ascended into heaven,
sitteth at the right hand of God the Father almighty;
from thence He shall come
to judge the living and the dead.

I believe in the Holy Ghost;
the holy Catholic Church;
the communion of Saints;
the forgiveness of sins;
the resurrection of the body,
and life everlasting.
Amen.

I believe in God,
the Father almighty,
Creator of heaven and earth.

God Beyond all Human Comprehension

God is incomprehensible. Nothing that we can comprehend is God. This is one of the essential characteristics of the nature of God. God is more sublime than any thoughts we can contrive about him. Even faith sees Him only in reflection and comparison. The Vatican Council says that "the divine mysteries by their own nature so far transcend the created intelligence that, even when delivered by revelation and received by faith, they remain covered with the veil of faith itself, and shrouded in a certain degree of darkness, so long as we are pilgrims in this mortal life, not yet with God; 'for we walk by faith and not by sight' (2 Corinthians 5:7)." Even in eternal life, when we shall see God face to face, no created being—not even the angels—shall be able to comprehend Him, to know Him exhaustively. Only God knows God entirely.

God is incomprehensible in all His attributes and in all His works. When we say "God is eternal" or "God is just" we approach the essence of God but very remotely. Our thought reaches out to Him, but it does not grasp Him. God's incomprehensibility becomes particularly obvious when we consider the history of the human race and of nations. Whoever acknowledges the existence of God must also acknowledge that God controls not only the course of history but every happening, big or small. Properly understood, this goes without saying. But there is no way to predict the workings of Divine Providence or to understand and explain them after the fact. Sacred Scripture (Isaias 55:8f.) states this most clearly: "Not mine, the Lord says, to think as you think, deal as you deal; by the full height of heaven above earth, my dealings are higher than your dealings, my thoughts than your thoughts."

Especially in times of historical change and upheaval the Christian should bear in mind that this incomprehensibility is of the very essence of God.

"Human understanding," wrote Novatian in the third century, "can form no worthy concept of God's essence nor of His magnitude nor of His attributes. The might of human language cannot bring forth a single word to express His majesty. All ingenuity of speech and all intellectual acumen are helpless before His greatness. Even sheer thought alone does not suffice to grasp Him; if it did He would be smaller than the mind of man, whereas in reality He is more sublime than any word, beyond any expression of ours. Everything which He Himself has thought, is less than Him. The totality of human speech, compared to Him is puny in the extreme. Turning to Him in silence we can, it is true, have some inkling of Him; but as to how He is in Himself, that is beyond our utterance. Call Him light, and you give a name rather to His creature than to Him. Call Him power, and you name not Him but that which is His. Call Him majesty, and you describe His glory rather than Him. He is more sublime than any sublimity, brighter than any light, stronger than any power, fairer than any beauty, truer than any truth, greater than all majesty. He is wiser than all wisdom, kinder than all loving kindness, more just than all justice! Name whatever force you choose, it will be less than Him who is the God and Father of all forces. Truly one can say: God is incomparable, God is beyond all that can be said."

The Blessed Trinity, Three Persons in One God

That God exists and that He is infinitely beyond all constructions of our imagination and of our reasoning is something which any man, even a pagan, can arrive at by his natural reason. He learns it from his observation of the world around him, from his own need for and experience of God, and from the teachings of his conscience. The natural and unaided reason of man, including pagan man, can also reach the knowledge that God in His omnipotence created the world and that in holiness and in the fullness of His might He now governs it.

But that God is Triune—which means that He is three divine persons in one divine nature—this is a mystery reserved to the believer alone. "No man has ever seen God," says St. John in his Gospel (1:18); "but now his only-begotten Son, who abides in the bosom of the Father, has himself become our interpreter." Jesus Christ revealed Himself as the Son of God the Father; and He sent us the Holy Spirit, through whom and in whom we are sanctified. Without the revelation of Jesus Christ nobody could have even the slightest inkling of the Blessed Trinity.

Now the mystery of the Trinity is a mystery to the believer too. It does not contradict reason but it lies above and beyond what reason can arrive at. On Trinity Sunday and on most Sundays throughout the year the Church declares this doctrine in the Preface of the Mass: "Right indeed it is, worthy and just, proper, and for our welfare, that we should always and everywhere give thanks to thee, holy Lord, almighty Father, eternal God; who with thy only-begotten Son and the Holy Ghost art one God, one Lord, not one as being a single person, but three Persons in one essence. Whatsoever by thy revelation we believe touching thy glory, that too we hold, without difference or distinction, of thy Son, and also of the Holy Spirit, so that in acknowledging the true, eternal Godhead, we adore in it each several Person, and yet a unity of essence, and a co-equal majesty."

Here is what one of the Fathers of the Church, St. Gregory Thaumaturgus (or Wonderworker), a bishop of the third century, says of the Blessed Trinity: "There is one God, Father of the living Word, Father of Him who is Wisdom, Power, and eternal Prototype. He is the perfect Begetter of the perfect Offspring, Father of the only-begotten Son. There is one Lord, only-begotten of the only God, as much God as His Begetter is, perfect reflection and identical image of the Godhead. He is the wholly effective creative Word, Wisdom comprehending all things, Power putting all creation into existence. He is true Son of true Father: as the Father is invisible, so He is invisible; as everlasting, so everlasting; as immortal, so immortal; as eternal, so eternal. And there is one Holy Spirit, a Person in the Divine Nature, and He appeared among men through the Son. He is the perfect replica of the full being of the Son; He is the living Giver of life, holy Source and Dispenser of holiness. In Him is God the Father revealed, who is above all things and in all things; and in Him is God the Son revealed, who is an exemplar for all things. These Three constitute a perfect Trinity in glory, eternity, and royal dominion, without division and without separate being. There is nothing created or subordinate in the Trinity, nor is there anything that might have been added later. There never was the Father without the Son, or the Son without the Spirit. Unchanging and unalterable the same Trinity is forever."

To this we add the words of St. Ephraem the Syrian: "Thou hast in the sun an image of the Father, in the sun's brightness an image of the Son, and in the sun's warmth an image of the Holy Spirit. Yet all this is one. Who will aspire to explain the incomprehensible?"

Many a Christian may ponder the mystery of the Blessed Trinity and come to the conclusion that while it certainly commands his honor and respect it is nevertheless too obscure and abstract to affect real life more than very slightly. The answer to this is that in a faith activated by love (of which there will be more to say later) the mystery becomes ever clearer and ever more effective in real life, even though it is never understood. Our evidence lies in the lives of the saints. Christ himself said that if any man loved Him he would win His Father's love (which is the Holy Spirit), and He and His Father would "come to him, and make our continual abode with him" (John 14:23). A life activated by faith, which is nothing less than a life of participation in the divine life of the Blessed Trinity itself, leads to an ever-growing understanding of the articles of faith. "The man whose life is true," says St. John (3:21), "comes to the light."

God the Father, the Creator

God the Father, the Unbegotten, the First Cause in the Trinity, is the Father of all creatures; and in a special way He is "Our Father," as Christ taught us to say. By His almighty love He called everything into existence—the heavens, the earth, visible beings, invisible beings, He created them all.

First, this article of faith means that the world, and above all man, do not derive their existence from themselves. Man and the world are both creatures, they are created, which means that they derive their existence from God. This fact is at the heart of the creation and of man; man's most essential characteristic is that he is a creature of God.

The words *creative* and *create* are often used rather loosely today. There is of course a legitimate use of the broad meaning of the terms, but strictly speaking only God is creative, because in the strict sense *to create* means *to bring forth out of nothing*. Where nothing was, God brought the world and man into existence. Nobody except God, neither the greatest artist nor the most profound thinker, can create something out of nothing. So everything except God was made from nothing and therefore constantly verges on nothingness; it depends wholly and constantly upon God's creative power and love to sustain it.

Second, this first article of the Creed means that God is before and above the world. He is altogether independent of the world, whereas the world is completely dependent upon Him. He is infinitely superior to the world, and in His being and His essence He is absolutely and unconditionally distinct from it. All this, however, does not mean that God is not present in the world and in all His creatures. Quite the contrary! He is present and works in all things. He is in us and is closer to us than we are to ourselves. "Where can I go, then, to take refuge from thy spirit, to hide from thy view? If I should climb up to heaven, thou art there; if I sink down to the world beneath, thou art present still. If I should take flight at dawn of day, and come to rest at the furthest ends of the sea, still would I find thee beckoning to me, thy right hand upholding me. Or perhaps I would think to bury myself in darkness; night should be the only witness of my pleasures; but no, darkness is no hiding-place from thee, with thee the night shines clear as the day itself; light and dark are one" (Psalms 138:7-12).

The process of creation of man and things never reaches a stage where man and things can exist solely of themselves and act solely of themselves. Rather God is constantly creating the world anew by conserving and sustaining all things in existence. But in no sense *is* the world God, neither as a whole nor in any of its parts. Nor is God in any way included in His creation. God's creative process in the world and in all beings stems from His complete sovereignty over the world. It is from God, utterly and completely above and outside the world, that all created beings and things derive their origin and their continued existence. By the creative power of God creation lives. All created things are infinitely distinct from the eternal and limitless God, their Creator. But God the Creator permeates everything with His divine essence and the allpowerfulness of His love.

The Ordered Structure of Creation

Creation is not a haphazard jumble of things and beings, but an organized structure ranging all the way from inorganic matter—the stones and rocks of this earth—to the angels before the face of God.

At the lowest level in this structure is inorganic matter. Plant life occupies the next higher level, visible to us in the flowers and trees. Plants take into their own life the environment in which they are rooted and by this they establish a link with the world. However, the relationship of plants to the world does not take place in the light of knowledge. Actual knowledge calls for the animal senses, and it is through these that animals draw into their lives a much larger portion of the world. Yet even the animal relationship to the world is incomplete, as it is limited to what the senses can reach, the surface element in things.

Penetration to the deeper essence of things, not perceptible to the senses, is possible only to the reasoning mind. The reasoning mind alone can relate itself to the whole of reality. To be able to establish an inner link with all creation is precisely what distinguishes the higher level on which man moves from the essentially lower level of the animal. Furthermore, only the reasoning mind is capable of an act of free will; and free will also distinguishes man essentially from all creatures lower than himself. Without freedom of choice and decision man could neither sin nor be converted nor be sanctified. However, the use of our mind requires the use of the senses to start with. Purely intellectual knowledge is not possible for man. Yet God so created our sensual-intellectual human nature as to make us able to see Him in the Beatific Vision in eternal life. The ultimate reason for man's distinctive difference is the spiritual character of his soul.

The fact that our mind cannot dispense with sense perception is what distinguishes us from the beings at the next higher level, the angels. An angel is a being of such superior keenness of intellect and such penetrating brilliance of mind that we should consider him as awesome rather than charming or pretty. By essence, angels are not the playmates of little children as popular imagination persists in picturing them; such a concept is not without beauty in its symbolic emphasis on the purity of the angels, but it does not reach the essential greatness of the angels. What puts the angels on a higher level than man is that they are bodiless spiritual beings completely independent of sense perceptions, who perceive and grasp the whole of creation much more directly and much more thoroughly than it is possible to the human mind.

Even so, man is the *center* of all creation—man, whose nature God Himself took upon Himself in Jesus Christ.

In man all levels and realms of the universe—spirit, animal, plant, inorganic matter—combine in an ordered unity.

God's Creation is Good

The Bible says, "And God saw all that he had made, and found it very good" (Gen. 1:31). All created things are good—even to this very day. And everything that necessarily follows from the divinely created essence of things is good. This is true not only of everything in the world outside of man and beneath man but also of man and of everything that necessarily follows from his being composed of body and soul—as, for example, begetting and multiplying, ruling the earth, directing and controlling the forces of nature, forming units of family, people, and state. The divinely created nature of the world is good in itself, the divinely created nature of man is good in itself. It needs neither justification nor apology. It is an act of injustice and contradiction against the Creator to disagree with Him and not find His creation good.

The Fall of the Angels and the Fall of Man

God created angels and man as free beings. This freedom, whether angelic or human, is so great that it can even turn against God Himself. This is one of the most obscure and impenetrable mysteries of the faith—that the very freedom which so images God in man and by which we can achieve the greatest likeness to God, can be abused for the entry of man upon paths contrary to God.

In perverse arrogance some of the angels actually did this. Because of this choice freely made—and for a purely spiritual being such a choice is irrevocable and final—

"Satan was cast down like a lightning flash from heaven" (Luke 10:18) and all his retinue with him. They fell from the Divine Presence down into regions of uttermost abandonment from God.

Man too abused his freedom. Seduced by Satan—who, though evil, still has a nature which is that of an angel and therefore superior to man's—man used his freedom to turn against his Creator.

At this point, in order to make all the far-reaching consequences of this abuse of freedom quite clear, we have to introduce another idea. Good as he was, in the sense that the earth itself and plants and animals were good and still are, the first man pleased God in an infinitely higher way than did all the other created beings on earth. Adam was more than good: he was holy. That is to say, he was filled with the Holy Spirit, he lived in supernatural community with God. The first man's community of life with God was a gift from God, a gift infinitely exceeding man's natural powers and anything due to man. What Adam's arrogant and ungodly choice primarily and especially destroyed was this very thing, his holiness, his supernatural life shared with God, in a word his "grace."

At the same time man also lost some other gifts of God, notably the effortless and automatic harmony of the various powers (or faculties) of his soul. The first sin obscured man's vision of truth, inclined his will to evil, and set his senses against his mind. This original sin is the root of suffering and disorder in the world, especially of bodily death.

Finally, it is through the fall of the angels and the fall of man that Satan became the "prince of this world" (see John 12:31, 14:30, 16:11). This does not mean that the world as such has become evil. The world as such ever remains the creation of God and therefore good. "Death was never of God's fashioning; not for his pleasure does life cease to be; what meant his creation, but that all created things should have being?" (Wisdom 1:14). But the forces of evil, the powers of the enemies of God, have acquired a might in the world. Worldly corruption is a force to be reckoned with because, as St. Peter warns us (2 Peter 2:19), "whatever influence gets the better of a man, becomes his master."

The Transmission of Original Sin

This deeply impaired human nature, cut off from the supernatural community of life with God by original sin, was transmitted in a mysterious manner by the first man to all his offspring through reproduction. By this very same process, God had willed that the *glory* of the first man was to have been transmitted to all the human race. The notion of such an "inheritance" is by no means foreign to present-day thinking. If people nowadays often find the doctrine of original sin an incongruous teaching not quite appropriate to the relationship between God and man, and even unworthy of it, this is mostly the result of misunderstanding.

In the first place, original sin in us is not a personal sinful act. Such an assertion would indeed be inappropriate and unrealistic. Original sin is not an act at all, it is a condition, or state. It is the condition of human nature separated from the supernatural community of life with God. As we have seen, this state of separation is contrary to the will of God and goes back to the personal sinful act of the first man. In some way or other all men have a share in it. It is a common guilt of mankind.

Secondly, the Church by no means teaches that original sin has rendered human nature wholly and fundamentally corrupt. On the contrary the Church expressly rejects this opinion as heresy. St. Thomas Aquinas, the "universal teacher" of the Church, was convinced that a man who dies burdened with no other sin than original sin can attain to a natural happiness in God, although he will remain excluded from supernatural union with Him. Even after original sin human nature remains basically and essentially good and capable of the good as long as a man does not of his own free will choose evil. And even if he does, human nature still retains its natural tendency to good.

More than this—not only did original sin not essentially corrupt man but the Church even calls it a "happy fault" —*felix culpa*—because it occasioned our redemption by Jesus Christ. Our Lord's act of redemption, restoring human nature from original sin and winning back for us what we had lost, has brought us something much greater than we could ever have lost. "And where sin abounded, grace did more abound" (Romans 5:20). Through Jesus Christ, who is "the way" to eternal life, a "new creation" was called into being. Man redeemed has become the brother and co-heir of the Son of God. This is why the Church begins one of her prayers in the Mass with the words, "O God, by whom the dignity of human nature was wondrously established and yet more wondrously restored."

And in Jesus Christ
His only Son our Lord;
who was conceived by the Holy Ghost,
born of the Virgin Mary,
suffered under Pontius Pilate,
was crucified, died, and was buried;
He descended into hell;
the third day He rose again from the dead;
He ascended into heaven.

The Son of God Became Man

The second part of the Creed speaks of Jesus Christ. Belief in Jesus Christ embraces two things: belief in the Incarnation (i.e., that God became Man), and belief in the Redemption (i.e., that God-become-Man redeemed us).

"The Word is born of the Father as a Son. The secret of His divine and holy birth was discovered by no Apostle, communicated to no prophet, come upon by no angel, perceived by no creature. To the Son alone it is and was ever apparent; the Son, who knows the secrets of the Father." And the Son has revealed it to His own. "None knows the Son truly except the Father, and none knows the Father truly except the Son, and those to whom it is the Son's good pleasure to reveal him." (Matthew 11:27). "In the beginning, before the foundation of the world, God begot unto Himself out of the well of His eternity and out of His divine and eternal Spirit His Son, the everlasting and true likeness of His own might and sublimity. This very Son is God's own Power and Intelligence, God's own Word and Wisdom." So speak two writers of the early Church—Novatian and Lactantius—on the mystery of the Eternal Word of God.

Now at a definite moment in human history the Second Person of the Blessed Trinity, the Eternal Word or the Son, took on a human nature. "The Word was made flesh" (John 1:14). This event is the center and turning point of all history. The division of history into a time "before Christ" and a time "after Christ" is basic. "It was [God's] loving design, centered in Christ, to give history its fulfillment by resuming everything in him, all that is in heaven, all that is on earth, summed up in him" (Ephesians 1:10).

When we say that God became Man we mean that the Eternal Word, unimpaired in the oneness of Its Person, took into Itself and upon Itself a human nature. Thus the nature of God and the nature of man are united in an indivisible Person; and the God who became Man in this way is Jesus Christ, who is both God and Man. This is to be understood not in some figurative sense but in the strictest and most literal sense. Christ is not "so to speak" God; He is truly God. He is not "so to speak" a man; He is truly Man, with body and soul. As God, Christ is of the same essence as the Father; and as Man, of the same essence as we. "There is one Lord, Jesus Christ, the only-begotten Word of the Father Himself, which became flesh without ceasing to be what It was. Even while Man, the Word remained God, and in the form of a servant It remained ruler. In emptying Itself It remained full of divinity, in weakness It remained Lord of all might, in the condition of humanity It remained sublime above all creation. For He retains forever what He possessed before He became flesh. He was God and true Son of God, Only-Begotten, Light, Life, Power.

And what He was not, this He took upon Himself when He made flesh His own on account of the divine decree of our salvation. . . . Christ was not first Man and then later God, but the Word was God and then became Man in order thus to be God and Man at one and the same time and in the same Person." Thus wrote St. Cyril of Alexandria.

In a sermon about the Passion of our Lord, Pope St. Leo the Great says: "Remaining God He did not disdain to take upon Himself the form of sinful flesh. Except for sin itself He took all our weaknesses which arise from sin. He underwent hunger and thirst, sleep and fatigue, grief and tears. Until the moment of His death He suffered the most cruel pains, and why? Because we could not be set free from the bonds of mortality if He did not let Himself be killed at the hands of godless men—He in whom alone the nature we all share was guiltless."

So it is just as accurate to say, "Christ is Almighty God," as it is to say, "Christ was led like a lamb to slaughter." The Eternal Word was born at a specific moment in history; and He who died on the Cross is the Almighty Himself.

On Christmas the Church sings in the Preface of the Mass as follows: "Through the mystery of the Word made flesh thy splendour has shone before our mind's eye with a new radiance, and through him whom we recognize as God made visible we are carried away in love of things invisible."

Mary, the Mother of God

Because divinity and humanity are so closely and directly joined in the Person of Jesus Christ, the Blessed

Virgin Mary really did "give birth to God" and she is truly and properly called the "Mother of God." The fact that she is God's mother, who conceived without union with man, by the overshadowing of the Holy Spirit—this great mystery raises Mary to her exalted rank high above any other being in human history and in all creation. For Mary was not a passive instrument chosen for divine motherhood. It is through her own decision and in full freedom of choice that she became the Mother of our Lord: "And Mary said, Behold the handmaid of the Lord; let it be unto me according to thy word" (Luke 1:38).

Mary is the only human being free from original sin and its consequences. It is to this circumstance—and not to the Virgin Birth of Christ—that the Church's teaching concerning the Immaculate Conception refers. Mary was *conceived* immaculate. By virtue of the Redemption which was to come through Jesus Christ, Mary, from the first moment of her existence, was in the state of grace, united to God in supernatural community of life. The dogma of Mary's bodily Assumption into heaven is a further development and unfolding of this truth.

The veneration which the Christian faithful have shown to Mary throughout the ages is due to her as the Mother of God. The Church never tires of singing the *Magnificat,* Mary's hymn of praise, recorded in St. Luke's Gospel (1: 46-55):

"My soul magnifies the Lord; my spirit has found joy in God, who is my Saviour, because he has looked graciously upon the lowliness of his handmaid. Behold, from this day forward all generations will count me blessed; because he who is mighty, he whose name is holy, has wrought for me his wonders. He has mercy upon those who fear him, from generation to generation; he has done valiantly with the strength of his arm, driving the proud astray in the conceit of their hearts; he has put down the mighty from their seat, and exalted the lowly; he has filled the hungry with good things, and sent the rich away empty-handed. He has protected his servant Israel, keeping his merciful design in remembrance, according to the promise which he made to our forefathers, Abraham and his posterity for evermore."

Redemption by Jesus Christ

The Incarnation completes and elevates all creation. For the very Prototype and Exemplar of all created beings, the Eternal Word of God, joined Itself most intimately with creation and so became creation's Head. The Son of God become Man is the Sacrament of sacraments. It is in Him that the Invisible God became visible for the sake of man's salvation, in the highest and most perfect fashion. The Redemption of man, which was consummated in Christ's death on the Cross, was first embodied in the Incarnation.

In the Creed of the Mass we say, "He for us men, and our salvation, came down from heaven," and the Preface for the Mass of the Epiphany speaks of "that restoration of our human nature which thy only-begotten Son accomplished when he put on mortality like ours and showed his immortality among us under a new light." To this we may add the words of St. Irenæus: "When the Son of God took flesh and became Man, He finished and completed the long development of humanity by putting himself at its head. This final act brought us our salvation, so that we regained in Christ Jesus what we had lost in Adam, namely our fullness of being—according to the image and likeness of God."

What does being restored and redeemed mean? Nothing less than being led back into the original supernatural community of life with God. Man could not have made this return on his own. Original sin had destroyed man's bridge of access to God, and only from God's side could the bridge be rebuilt. Jesus Christ rebuilt it. He led man back to his original holiness, his original friendship with God. Jesus Christ gave us the Holy Spirit once more —whom the sin of the first man had lost for all of us. In this way Christ also freed us from the rule of Satan, of whom Sacred Scripture (John 12:31) tells us that he was "cast out" by reason of the redeeming sacrifice of Jesus Christ.

As for the other consequences of original sin, they still remain with us even after the Redemption—especially our internal conflict, our suffering, our physical death. But these things have now become transformed into healing remedies conducive to eternal life. In his own suffering, man is able to take part in the redeeming suffering of Christ—a suffering which the Church calls blessed. In his Epistle to the Colossians (1:24) St. Paul says, "Even as I write, I am glad of my sufferings on your behalf, as, in this mortal frame of mine, I help to pay off the debt which the afflictions of Christ leave still to be paid, for the sake of his body, the Church."

As we have seen, the essential nature of the Redemption, by which sinful humanity was retrieved, is to lead man back to friendship—indeed to sonship—with God. Redemption, however, must not be conceived as the fruit of Christ's teaching alone, though this teaching is infinitely superior in truth and depth to any human wisdom. Neither is it the result of the Lord's example in His life and His works, though this example is infinitely superior to any human leadership. No, Redemption was effected by

God's becoming Man, suffering, and sacrificing Himself voluntarily on the Cross, even unto death. Our Lord Himself said of Himself (Mark 10:45) that He came "to give his life as a ransom for the lives of many." And St. Peter wrote in his First Epistle (1 Peter 1:18-19), "You know well enough that [your ransom] was not paid in earthly currency, silver or gold; it was paid in the precious blood of Christ; no lamb was ever so pure, so spotless a victim."

The Redemption Beyond Our Understanding

Even though we are able to understand that man could not be redeemed except through Jesus Christ, and even though Fathers and Doctors of the Church have explained this necessity and in manifold thoughts and figures of speech so interpreted the work of Christ, the full and true nature of the Incarnation and the Redemption both remain beyond human comprehension. What St. Hilary of Poitiers said about the generation of the Eternal Word we may equally well apply to the Eternal Word's Incarnation: "I do not know, nor do I enquire, but yet I find consolation. The archangels do not know it, the angels do not learn it, the millennia do not contain it, the prophetic spirit did not proclaim it, the Apostle did not ask it, the Son Himself has not relinquished it. Will you then, who do not know the origin of creation, not endure in quiet humility your ignorance about the birth of the Creator?"

The Council of Trent issued a catechism in which we read: "Indeed, if one thing more than another presents difficulty to the mind and understanding of man, assuredly it is the mystery of the cross, which, beyond all doubt, must be considered the most difficult of all; so much so that only with great difficulty can we grasp the fact that our salvation depends on the cross, and on Him who for us was nailed thereon." [1]

Yet this is truly so. In the Preface for Passiontide the Church prays: "Holy Lord, almighty Father, eternal God! By thy ordinance the salvation of mankind was accomplished on the wood of the Cross, so that life might rise again there where death had its beginning, and that he who conquered through a tree should on a tree himself be conquered: through Christ our Lord."

Our Lord's Death on the Cross

Jesus Christ really died on the Cross. His soul really left His body. His dead body was taken down from the Cross and buried, and it is certainly no accident that the Creed enumerates these happenings one by one, "was crucified, died, and was buried." By these words, and by the precise indication of the time of the Passion—"under Pontius Pilate"—the declaration is made to all the world that Christ's act of Redemption happened at a definite time in history in the land of Palestine.

His Descent into Hell

What is called Christ's descent "to those in the underworld" is the event which brought the fruits and benefits of Redemption to those who had lived and died before the time of Christ. To all who had obeyed God and believed in Him as best they knew, Christ brought Redemption, raising them to eternal community of life with God. "We cannot know," says St. Jerome, "how the Blood of

[1] *Catechism of the Council of Trent for Parish Priests,* translated into English with notes by John A. McHugh, O.P., and Charles J. Callan, O.P. New York (Wagner), 10th printing, 1947. p. 52.

Christ helped those in the underworld. Yet that it was of use to them, this we must know."

His Resurrection from the Dead

Christ completed His redemptive work in His Resurrection from the dead. This is what overcame the frailty of human nature; and only with the Resurrection was the full fruit of the Redemption revealed—eternal life of the whole man, in God. Hence Easter, the feast of the Resurrection, is properly also the actual feast of the Redemption. St. Paul says (1 Corinthians 15:17) that "if Christ has not risen, all your faith is a delusion; you are back in your sins." And again (Romans 4:24-25): "It will be reckoned virtue in us, if we believe in God as having raised our Lord Jesus Christ from the dead: handed over to death for our sins, and raised to life for our justification." The Church says (Preface for the Mass of Easter) that Christ "by dying has brought our death to naught, and by rising again has restored us to life."

His Ascension into Heaven

After His Resurrection Christ entrusted some important teachings to the Apostles. The Book of Acts (1:3) says that He was "telling them about the kingdom of God." His special promise to them was that the Holy Spirit would come; repeating this promise to them now, forty days after His Resurrection from the dead, He charged them to make all the peoples of the earth His disciples. Then before their eyes He ascended into heaven—in order (as the Preface for Ascension says) "that he might grant us fellowship in his Godhead." St. Leo the Great says, "Christ's Ascension is our exaltation. Whither the transfigured Head has gone, thither it is the hope of all flesh to go."

Jesus Christ, Priest and Lord

We have seen that the Incarnation and the Redemption are the two mysteries of our faith which provide the basis of our relationship to Jesus Christ. He is our mediator and advocate with God. As mediator, Jesus Christ is first and foremost Priest. From His Priesthood all other priesthood in the world is derived. To be a priest is to offer sacrifice to God for men and to distribute among men the gifts of God's grace. —"The purpose for which any high priest is chosen from among his fellow-men, and made a representative of men in their dealings with God, is to offer gifts and sacrifices in expiation of their sins" (Hebrews 5:1). But the sacrifice which Jesus Christ offered—"to drain the cup of a world's sins" (Hebrews 9:28)—was Himself. "Son of God though he was, he learned obedience in the school of suffering, and now, his full achievement reached, he wins eternal salvation for all those who render obedience to him. A high priest in the line of Melchisedech, so God has called him" (Hebrews 5:8-10).

Christ is not only Priest, He is also Head and Lord of the whole human race. God "has put everything under his dominion, and made him the head to which the whole Church is joined, so that the Church is his body, the completion of him who everywhere and in all things is complete" (Ephesians 1:22).

He sitteth at the right hand of God the Father almighty;
from thence He shall come
to judge the living and the dead.

Christ's Work Ever Present

The life and work of Jesus Christ did not stop with the Ascension. The life of Jesus Christ on earth is not a thing of the past but a living reality continued into the presence and the future. In the words of St. Paul (Hebrews 13:8), "what Jesus Christ was yesterday, and is today, he remains for ever."

The union of two Natures in one Person—divine and human in Christ—endures today and eternally. "Jesus continues for ever" (Hebrews 7:24). The self-sacrifice of the Redemption, furthermore, although it happened only once and at a single moment in history, is constantly being renewed in the present; for this is the Sacrifice of the Mass offered by the Holy Church in which Jesus Christ continues to live.

The Creed's way of calling attention to Christ's transcendence of history is by changing the tense. Up to and including the Ascension the tenses are in the past—historical. But He "*sitteth* at the right hand of God the Father almighty" is present—eternal.

"Sitting at the right hand of God" must not be taken in a literal, bodily sense. It simply means that the glorified Christ, still Man as well as God, has taken permanent possession of His highest kingship and highest kingly glory. This is the truth St. Paul prayed we should understand when he wrote (Ephesians 1:18-21): "May your inward eye be enlightened, so that you may understand to what hopes [God] has called you, how rich in glory is that inheritance of his found among the saints, what surpassing virtue there is in his dealings with us, who believe. Measure it by that mighty exercise of power which he shewed when he raised Christ from the dead, and bade him sit on his right hand above the heavens, high above all princedoms and powers and virtues and dominations, and every name that is known, not in this world only, but in the world to come." God has put Jesus Christ, the Son of Man, higher than the choirs of angels: "Did he ever say to one of the angels, Sit on my right hand?" (Hebrews 1:13).

The Second Coming of our Lord

At the end of the world Jesus Christ will come again, and His glory as ruler will become visible to all creatures. At His first coming, in the womb of the Mother of God and in His birth at Bethlehem, our Lord's divinity remained hidden. Since then the history of His kingdom has been unfolding upon earth, and it will continue to do so until the second coming on the last day of the world. This will be the return of the Son of Man, Jesus Christ, whose divinity and glorified humanity will shine forth in bright and unmistakable radiance. "And then," says St. Mark (14:26), "they will see the Son of Man coming upon the clouds, with great power and glory." And this coming of Christ will be in *judgment*—judgment upon all mankind, upon all individual men, upon all peoples, upon the whole world in all its history. Sacred Scripture says that "when the Son of Man comes in his glory, and all the angels with him, he will sit down upon the throne of his glory, and all nations will be gathered in his presence, where he will divide men one from the other, as the shepherd divides the sheep from the goats; he will set the sheep on his right, and the goats on his left. Then the King will say to those who are on his right hand, Come, you that have received a blessing from my Father, take possession of the kingdom which has been prepared for you since the foundation of the world. . . . Then he will say to those who are on his left hand, in their turn, Go far from me, you that are accursed, into that eternal fire which has been prepared for the devil and his angels" (Matthew 25:31-34, 41).

This judgment of the whole world will be the most public judgment imaginable. It will be carried out in the sight of all the peoples and generations of men, and in the presence of all creation. It is entirely in accord with man's own healthy impulse to see justice done that the wicked will be punished and the good rewarded before the eyes of the whole world. Before this judgment, immediately after the death of each individual human being, there is a non-public particular judgment, in which each individual human being hears the sentence passed upon his personal life. This sentence is absolutely just and therefore irrevocable. The Judge at both judgments is the same—Jesus Christ, God become Man, who said of Himself (John 5:27) that the Father has "granted him power to execute judgment, since he is the Son of Man."

The Church's Portrait of Christ

We have seen the Christ of the Creed, a Christ beyond our comprehension yet unmistakably clear: "Visible God" come near to man, yet quite beyond our grasp in the depth and height of the union of divinity and humanity in Him. We close our exposition of the second part of the Creed with two comprehensive presentations of the Church's portrait of Christ. In both of them it is well to remember that explaining a mystery is something like making darkness shine.

The first is from a letter of Pope St. Leo IX (1049-54): "I believe in the Son of God the Father, the Word of God born of the Father in eternity before all time, whose divinity in every respect—whether of being, omnipotence, or perfection—equals that of the Father. He was born in time of Mary ever Virgin, in whom He was conceived of the Holy Spirit. He is twice born, once in eternity of the Father, once in time of His Mother. He has two wills and two modes of operation. He is true God and true Man, unique and complete in each of the two Natures. He is the sole and only God. He is the Son of God in two Natures, but in the uniqueness of His one Person. In His divinity He was incapable of suffering, and immortal. In His humanity He endured for us and for our salvation real bodily sufferings. He was buried, and on the third day thereafter He really rose from the dead, body and soul. In corroboration of this He ate with His disciples. On the fortieth day after His Resurrection He ascended into heaven with His risen body and His soul. He sits at the right hand of the Father. From there on the tenth day he sent the Holy Spirit. And from there He will come as He ascended, in order to judge the living and the dead and to reward every man according to his works."

The other portrait is from the Apocalypse (or Revelation), the most obscure book of the Bible. Its approach is that of prophetic vision, and in the first chapter (1:13-18) this is how the Son of Man appears: "I saw seven golden candlesticks, and in the midst of these seven golden candlesticks one who seemed like a son of man, clothed in a long garment, with a golden girdle about his breast. The hair on his head was like wool snow-white, and his eyes like flaming fire, his feet like orichalc melted in the crucible, and his voice like the sound of water in deep flood. In his right hand were seven stars; from his mouth came a sword sharpened at both its edges; and his face was like the sun when it shines at its full strength. At the sight of him, I fell down at his feet like a dead man; and he, laying his right hand on me, spoke thus: Do not be afraid; I am before all, I am at the end of all, and I live."

I believe in the Holy Ghost;
the holy Catholic Church;
the communion of Saints;
the forgiveness of sins;
the resurrection of the body,
and life everlasting.
Amen.

The Work of the Holy Spirit

The third and last part of the Creed treats of the fruit of our Redemption—the Holy Spirit and His sanctifying work. Each of the three divine Persons is spirit, and each is holy. Yet the Third Person of the Trinity is especially designated by the name Holy Ghost, or Holy Spirit. As we saw in our treatment of the Blessed Trinity, St. Gregory the Wonderworker expresses the Creed's teaching on the Holy Spirit as follows: "And there is one Holy Spirit, a Person in the Divine Nature, and He appeared among men through the Son. He is the perfect replica of the full being of the Son; He is the living Giver of life, holy Source and Dispenser of holiness." The Church says that the Holy Spirit is the bond of love which embraces the Father and the Son and proceeds from them both. St. Augustine says that "as the Word of God is the Son of God, so the Love of God is the Holy Spirit." And St. Paul says (Romans 5:5) that "the love of God has been poured out in our hearts by the Holy Spirit, whom we have received."

The Holy Spirit is the "giver of life," as the Creed of the Mass says: "I believe too in the Holy Spirit, Lord and life-giver." He enlivens the souls of men with love. Love is what He is. In the infinite completeness of His Person

He is what binds the soul of man supernaturally to God, the absolute First Cause of life. Through this supernatural love man is made a saint and a son of God. Thus as the Father creates man and the Son redeems him, so the Holy Spirit sanctifies him, makes him holy. Through the work of the Holy Spirit, who is the focus of all supernatural life, Creation and Redemption are brought to their completion. St. Paul (Galatians 4:6) says that it is the presence of the Holy Spirit in us that enables us to call God "Father"; and it is therefore the Holy Spirit who makes us true sons of God. Man, created by God the Father and redeemed by Jesus Christ, is sanctified and strengthened by the Holy Ghost, even to the point of martyrdom. "It is the Holy Ghost," says Novatian, "who strengthens the hearts and minds of men, who illumines the Gospel mysteries, and who sets the deeds of God in their proper light. Those who have been strengthened by Him have shown fear of neither chains nor dungeons for the sake of the Lord; for they carried within them the gifts of this Spirit—the same gifts with which He has adorned the Church, His Bride."

The Holy Spirit in the Church of Christ

At the Council of Nicæa (325 A.D.) the Church declared that the Holy Spirit dwells within her. Christ had promised the Apostles that the Holy Spirit would come as their "Advocate" and "Comforter." "But when the Advocate has come, whom I will send you from the Father, the Spirit of truth who proceeds from the Father, he will bear witness concerning me. . . . But when he, the Spirit of truth, has come, he will teach you all the truth" (John 15:26; 16:13).

On the first Pentecost (or Whitsunday) the Holy Spirit was sent to the young Church, as our Lord had promised. At this moment the Church entered definitely upon her full life. St. Thomas Aquinas says that the Holy Ghost is the soul of the Church, and just as a man's body is animated by his soul, so the Church lives by virtue of the Holy Spirit whom Christ sent to her in the power of the Father.

The Church, the People of God

The English word *church* (like the German *Kirche*) comes from the Greek *kyriaké*, meaning *she who belongs to the Lord.* The first Christians called the church the community of God on earth, and that is what she is: the People of God. In Sacred Scripture she rejoices in many names: the House of God, the Pillar and Foundation of Truth, the Fold of the Flock of Christ—to which Christ is both Gate and Shepherd. She is called the Bride of Christ and the Bride of the Holy Ghost. And finally she is the very Body of Christ.

The Church, unlike other communities and societies of men, was not founded by men. True enough, men constitute her; but they did not make her. The Church, the People of God, was founded by Jesus Christ, that is by God Himself. The Roman Catechism says that God called men into the Church through the inner working of the Holy Spirit who opens the hearts of men. Accordingly the power of rule by which the Church is governed is not of human origin; its origin is divine. This power goes back to the call of St. Peter by Jesus Christ, and it works out its effects by the power of the Holy Spirit, who is the soul and life of the Church. This is why the true nature of the Church cannot be grasped by the natural cognitive powers alone. Although the Church is visible, and although her "administrative measures" appear not to differ substantially from those of other societies of men, the real basis of her life and the core of her being are visible to the eyes of faith only. For she is the Church of Christ.

The Holiness of the Church

The Creed expressly calls the Church "holy," just as the Book of Acts (9:32; 26:10) speaks of the Christians as "the saints"—that is to say the holy ones. By Christians and non-Christians alike this word *holy* is frequently misunderstood in the application that the Creed here makes of it. The Creed does not mean to say that all the faithful are holy people, or that all priests are. Nor does the unholiness of members or officials of the Church impair the holiness of the Church. We have it on the frequent and emphatic word of Jesus Christ Himself that good and evil exist side by side in the Church. There are numerous parables to this effect. The Gospel compares the Church to a net cast into the sea and drawn out full of fish of all kinds, good and bad; or to a field in which weeds grow in the midst of the good grain; or to a threshing floor of wheat and chaff. Yet in her essential nature the Church is holy. Her holiness consists in this, that the Holy Spirit lives and works in her, that she and only she can offer the holy Sacrifice of Jesus Christ, and that she and only she has the power to administer the sacraments of the New Covenant, the new and living channels of divine sanctifying grace.

The Church is holy because she is the Body of Christ—Christ who suffered and died to "sanctify the people through his own blood" (Hebrews 13:12). There is no need to say that this holiness of the Church does both call and oblige all members of the Church to a holy life. The

Church, as Church, is holy; but every single Christian should also be a means whereby the fruit of the Redemption is brought to himself and to others through the holiness of his own life. Now a part of the Church definitely is holy in this everyday sense of the word—even leaving aside the many holy Christians in this world, both hidden and obvious. We mean the saints in heaven, those who have already attained eternal life. To distinguish them from the "Church Militant" still striving on earth, they are called the "Church Triumphant." For them the strife has ended—in victory.

The Communion of Saints

The expression *Communion of Saints* is not just another name for the Church Triumphant. Nor does it designate—primarily and exclusively—the communion between the Church on earth and the saints in heaven. Nor, finally, is it to be taken as synonymous with the words *Holy Catholic Church,* even when these are understood in their widest sense as including all members of the Church in heaven (The Church Triumphant), on earth (The Church Militant), and in purgatory (The Church Suffering). Communion of Saints is a more comprehensive expression in that it designates the common bond uniting all members of the whole Church, Christ's Mystical Body, in this world and the next. This common bond of union between Christ and His holy Mother and all the saints of heaven and all members of the Church on earth and all the "poor souls" in purgatory—this bond consists in a real and mutual communication of spiritual riches. What belongs to one belongs to all. All members of this communion—all just souls of whatever time and place, including all honest believers in Christ and honest seekers after God who may be said to be members of the Church "in desire" only—all share in the holy "common property" of the Sacrifice of Jesus Christ and of the sacraments of Jesus Christ. In explaining the Communion of Saints the Roman Catechism says: "The fruit of all the sacraments accrues to the faithful as a whole and to all of them; by means of the sacraments, as by a sacred bond, they are bound to Christ and united with Him." To which we may add the words of St. Thomas's commentary on the Creed: "Everything good which the saints ever brought about is imparted to those who live in Charity, because they are all one. 'I am a partaker,' says the Psalmist (Psalms 118:63), 'with all them that fear thee.' "

Out of this concept of the Communion of Saints grows the veneration of the saints, the prayer for their intercession, and our own intercessory prayer for the poor souls in purgatory.

The Forgiveness of Sins

For man on earth, the first fruit of this community of grace with Christ is the forgiveness of his sins through baptism and penance. Sin is willful and conscious turning away from God. Sin is still as possible to commit after the Redemption as it was before; the grace of Redemption is not compelling, man's will remains free. Nor did the Redemption put a stop to the human will's inclination to evil, one of the consequences of original sin. But through the Redemption we have been given the possibility of wholly effacing even the heaviest guilt—provided that we submit ourselves in repentance to the healing judgment of Christ in His Church. "Receive the Holy Spirit," said Christ to the Apostles (John 20:22-23); "when you forgive men's sins, they are forgiven, when you hold them bound, they are held bound." This full authoritative power to forgive sins in the name of God and in the power of the Holy Spirit is something that was never entrusted to any man in all the ages before the birth of Christ.

The Resurrection of the Body

The Holy Spirit, as St. Thomas puts it, sanctifies the Church not only in the souls of the faithful by forgiving their sins and imparting sanctifying grace, but "through His power our bodies also will rise again." It is the belief of the Church of Christ that at the end of time and of this world all people will rise bodily from the dead. "The time is coming," said Christ (John 5:28-30), "when all those who are in their graves will hear [the voice of the Son of Man] and will come out of them; those whose actions have been good, rising to new life, and those whose doings have been evil, rising to meet their sentence."

How this is to happen, or what the resurrected body will be like,—this no man can know or say. The Apostle Paul gave his answer to questions of this kind in the first Epistle to the Corinthians (1 Corinthians 15:35-38): "But perhaps someone will ask, How can the dead rise up? What kind of body will they be wearing when they appear? Poor fool, when thou sowest seed in the ground, it must die before it can be brought to life; and what thou sowest is not the full body that is one day to be; it is only bare grain, of wheat, it may be, or some other crop; it is for God to embody it according to his will, each grain in the body that belongs to it."

One thing, however, is now certain—that for those who die in communion with Christ these words of Sacred Scripture (1 Corinthians 15:42-44) will come to pass: "What is sown corruptible, rises incorruptible; what is sown unhonoured, rises in glory; what is sown in weakness, is raised in power; what is sown a natural body, rises a spiritual body."

Eternal Life

The Church's name for this "incorruptible glory" is *eternal life.* There all our unrest comes to rest, all our longing is satisfied in blessed and beneficent union with the Blessed Trinity. What we have said of all the other articles of faith holds true also—and especially—of this last one. "I believe in life everlasting" expresses a mystery which no man will ever fully grasp as long as he lives on this earth. In the first of his three Epistles (1 John 3:2) St. John says that "we are sons of God even now, and what we shall be hereafter, has not been made known as yet. But we know that when he comes we shall be like him; we shall see him, then, as he is." And St. Paul (1 Corinthians 2:9) tells us that "no eye has seen, no ear has heard, no human heart conceived, the welcome God has prepared for those who love him."

The Punishment of the Damned

What of those who do not love God? For them, if they persist in turning from Him even unto death, there is a place of torture prepared; and the bitterness of this place consists in the very thing which they who go there wished to have during their earthly life—namely, separation from God. Irrevocable unbridgeable remoteness from God is the essence of eternal punishment for sin; that this remoteness is senseless and perverse becomes instantly, fully, and relentlessly clear to the soul that is damned, together with the realization that it is irrevocable.

The Christian, then, believes in the Triune God and in His threefold work of Creation, Redemption, and Sanctification.

But this threeness of the divine Persons and the threefold division of their divine works should not dim our awareness of the unity and uniqueness of God nor of the unity and common origin of all His works. There is but one Divine Nature—God is One. And this One indivisible God is the originator of all His works.

God the Father is in a special sense the Creator; yet it is the Son of whom we say in the Creed of the Mass, "through whom all things were made"; and it is the Holy Spirit to whom we sing on Pentecost, "Come, Holy Ghost, Creator."

The work of Redemption is attributed primarily to the Son and in a very special way is properly His since it was in His person that the two natures were united. Yet in the Mass the priest prays, "Lord Jesus Christ, Son of the living God, who, by the Father's will and the co-operation of the Holy Spirit, didst by thy death bring life to the world."

Of the Holy Spirit, to whom is attributed the work of Sanctification, Christ Himself said that this is He "whom the Father will send on my account" (John 14:26).

The true revealed meaning of the God Who is One and Three is summed up by the theologian Hirscher: "What the Father is to us and gives to us, He is and gives through the Son, in the Holy Spirit; no one has the Father except in the Son, and no one confesses the Son except in the Holy Spirit."

The Christian submits himself and his existence to the activating power of this one, mysterious, Triune God in making the sign of the Cross, pronouncing, in union with the whole Church, the ancient and solemn prayer:

"Glory be to the † Father, and to the † Son, and to the † Holy Ghost; as it was in the beginning, is now, and ever shall be, world without end. Amen."

THE LIFE OF THE CHRISTIAN

Our Share in the Life of the Blessed Trinity

The belief of the Christian is belief in the Triune God and in His threefold work of Creation, Redemption, and Sanctification. But as we said at the start, belief is only one of the two things setting Christians apart from other men. The other is the life stemming from this belief.

Belief (or faith) is the foundation, root, and beginning of life. Whoever believes without living his belief—particularly in active love for God and neighbor—is as an unfinished structure. St. Ignatius of Antioch, holy bishop and martyr of the early Church, wrote in one of his letters: "You will lack nothing if in full measure you have faith and love for Jesus Christ. These things are the beginning and the purpose of life—for the beginning is faith, but the purpose is love. Both of them, bound together in one unity, come from God. Everything pertaining to perfection flows from them." And St. Paul expresses the same idea: "I may have powers of prophecy, no secret hidden from me, no knowledge too deep for me; I may have utter faith, so that I can move mountains; yet if I lack charity, I count for nothing" (1 Corinthians 13:2).

The Blessed Trinity is the cornerstone of both the belief and the life of the Christian. Life activated by Christian faith consists in the Christian's cooperation in the works of the Blessed Trinity. The central purpose of this life is that, sanctified by the Holy Spirit, we allow the creative work of the Father and the redemptive work of the Son to become fruitful and complete in us. The life of the

Christian is participation in the life of the Blessed Trinity.

This share in the life of the Trinity is what we call *sanctifying grace,* a term frequently misunderstood but having no other meaning than this—the life of God as shared by us. The word *grace* (that is, free gift) is sometimes misinterpreted as an offense to man's natural dignity and self-respect. But this is not the case. As Sacred Scripture records (Wisdom 12:18), God uses "great reverence" in disposing our ways. Assuredly, sanctifying grace is something to which we have no claim by nature. It is utterly and completely a free gift of God. But at the same time it is truly an elevation, which man merits by reason of the suffering and death of Jesus Christ, who is both God and Man; it lifts human nature into the Divine Nature, in order to live a life proceeding from the Holy Spirit, the threefold life of God Himself. Thus Christ has made us true children of God. From the Apostle John we have the great reminder (1 John 3:1) that we are "called children of God; and such we are." Even the natural goods we enjoy—health, happiness, beauty, strength—are in a certain sense grace, since they are gifts of God to man; but in the strict sense grace means the new life of divine sonship which Christ brought us and which will unfold in all its fullness in eternal life.

This supernatural community of life with the Trinity we receive through the sacraments of the Church of Jesus Christ. So the life of the Christian is first and foremost the sacramental life in and with the Church. Sanctifying grace then grows and progresses in us because of good works of ours which proceed from our supernatural state as children of God and from real virtue—that is, from our firm direction to good, in which we are strengthened and confirmed by grace. It is necessary here to point out that the virtues cannot be acquired by man alone without the sanctifying grace of God; nor can man of his own power keep sanctifying grace in his possession if God does not continually help him.

In this second section of this book, therefore, we shall deal with two things: the life of the Christian with the Church, and the virtues of the Christian.

THE LIFE OF THE CHRISTIAN WITH THE CHURCH

THE SEVEN SACRAMENTS

The Sacraments and the New Life

The life of the Christian with the Church consists first and foremost in active participation in her sacramental life; for it is through the sacraments that sanctifying grace lays the first foundations of the new life which a Christian enjoys as a son of God. The Council of Trent says that "through the sacraments all true holiness is begun, increased, and—if it has been lost—regained." In the sacraments new life flows into the Christian by the power of the Holy Spirit, who is the soul of the Church and the giver of her life.

The Sacrament of all sacraments is the Incarnation, and the seven sacraments of the Church are both its fruit and its image. Just as in Jesus Christ invisible God took on a visible body, so the new life which He won for us by becoming Man and dying on the Cross became tangible and visible for us in the sacraments of the Church. The body of a sacrament is the outward sign to which Christ himself attached the winning and receiving of the new life of grace.

How the New Life Grows in the Seven Sacraments

This new life begins and grows in a Christian in a pattern similar to that of his bodily life. Our bodily life begins as a result of natural begetting and birth. Our new life begins with supernatural birth—*baptism.*

Natural man keeps growing until his body reaches full maturity. The maturity of his new life is conferred on him by *confirmation.*

Our bodily life demands nourishment. The nourishment of our new life is the *Holy Eucharist,* the Body of our Lord, made present and offered up in the Holy Sacrifice of the Mass and received in Holy Communion. This Most Holy Sacrament of the Altar is also known simply as the *Blessed Sacrament.*

When injury and illness threaten our natural life, we draw upon our inner healing forces to overcome them. The new life has a healing force too, which works through the sacraments of *penance* and *extreme unction.* The sacrament of penance heals the soul from the injury left by sin, and more especially it restores the new life after mortal sin has destroyed it. The sacrament of extreme unction (or last anointing), given to those who are gravely ill, strengthens the new life for entrance into eternity and purifies it of any of the remnants of sin. It very often happens that extreme unction restores bodily health as well.

Our natural life owes its continued existence to the family and the state: man is born in a family and grows into a citizen under the ordered and lawful protection of the civil community. Propagation and protection of the new life are provided for by the sacraments of *holy orders* and *matrimony.* By the power which bishops and priests have to administer the sacraments, the new life is perpetuated in God's own people, the Church; while through the various degrees of jurisdiction in the priestly hierarchy this people is given order, stability, and direction. In Christian marriage, or matrimony, man and woman come together to bring forth young natural life destined to the service of God in the world.

Birth into the new life takes place at baptism. This new birth restores to man his supernatural community of life with the Blessed Trinity and wipes out the stain of the first sin of man, inherited through natural generation. This stain is washed away by the sanctified water which is poured over the person being baptized, and this pouring is done expressly in the name of the Blessed Trinity—in the name of the Father, and of the Son, and of the Holy Ghost. In the early Church, baptism was performed by immersion. This, as St. Thomas among others points out, represented our entering into life with Christ by being buried with him. "In our baptism," says St. Paul (Romans 6:4), "we have been buried with him, died like him, that so, just as Christ was raised up by his Father's power from the dead, we too might live and move in a new kind of existence."

This first sacrament lays the foundation for the others by making us sharers in the new life of sanctifying grace and members of the Body of Christ. This membership in Christ is irrevocable and undying. By his actions or express decision of will a man may repudiate it, nevertheless he belongs once and for all to Christ. While one can renounce membership in the visible community of the Church, one cannot in this way or in any way erase the mark of Christ with which the soul has been sealed at baptism; nor can one renounce the obligation which this mark has set up.

In baptism we become temples of the Holy Spirit, members of the Body of Christ, branches of the Vine that is Christ. Baptism gives a Christian the right to offer the Holy Sacrifice of the Mass in union with the priest and to receive the Body of our Lord in Holy Communion.

Baptism opens the way to all the other sacraments of the Church of Jesus Christ, and it likewise entitles us to a part in all her blessings and prayers. Finally, by baptism man is made capable and worthy of eternal life. St. Methodius, an early Father of the Eastern Church, boldly states that "those who have been enlightened by baptism acquire the traits, likeness, and manhood of Christ; for in the baptized the image of the Word is stamped, and by deep knowledge and complete faith it is born in them, so that Christ Himself begins to live spiritually in each of them."

The Sacrament of Confirmation

In the sacrament of confirmation our new life arrives at maturity and full strength; for confirmation is the sacrament of coming of age, of entry into the ranks of adult Christians. Every one who has been confirmed is a full-fledged member of the Church Militant and has both the right and the duty of sharing responsibility with and for all the other members. Irrevocably and ineffaceably, this sacrament stamps the awakening personality of the young Christian at its very center and forms it throughout by the power of the Holy Spirit, in order that from now on his life, which he guides by his own free will and choice, may be sanctified.

The maturity of the new life manifests itself especially in a Christian's manly and firm power of decision, and in his readiness to acknowledge Christ and fight for him. The power of "boldly confessing the name of Christ" is a power divinely conferred. The Church calls it the most excellent of the fruits of confirmation.

Normally, only the bishop is empowered to administer this sacrament. He lays his hands on the head of the young Christian (just as he does when ordaining a priest) and signs his forehead with the sign of the Cross, anointing it with holy oil (chrism). While doing so he says, "I sign thee with the sign of the Cross and fortify thee with the oil of salvation, in the Name of the Father and of the Son and of the Holy Ghost." The Council of Florence explains that "the Christian is anointed on the forehead, which is the seat of shame, so that he will not blush to bear witness to Christ or to the Cross with which he is signed; for as St. Paul says (1 Corinthians 1:23), the Cross is 'to the Jews a discouragement, to the Gentiles mere folly.' "

The Holy Eucharist

In baptism and confirmation a Christian becomes a sharer in the power of Christ. In the Holy Eucharist not only the power of Christ is present, but Christ Himself—He is the offering Priest, the offering, and the sacrificial meal. Christ Himself is the nourishment through which the new life is maintained in the Christian. Accordingly Christ is present in the Sacrament under the appearance of bread, the nourishment of natural life.

At the moment in the Mass when the priest consecrates the bread and wine so that they become the Divine Food, the Body and Blood of our Lord, he speaks the words our Lord spoke on the evening before His Passion, when He performed this marvelous mystery for the first time. "FOR THIS IS MY BODY." "FOR THIS IS THE CHALICE OF MY BLOOD, OF THE NEW AND EVERLASTING COVENANT, A MYSTERY OF FAITH. IT SHALL BE SHED FOR YOU AND MANY OTHERS, SO THAT SINS MAY BE FORGIVEN."

The Holy Eucharist (called also the Sacrament of the Altar, or the Blessed Sacrament) is the greatest of all the sacraments, and the center of all the others. Baptism makes us fit to receive the Body of our Lord; so do penance (after serious sin) and extreme unction. Confirmation strengthens this fitness. The sacrament of holy orders enables the ordained priest to celebrate the Eucharist in Holy Mass and to distribute It in the Communion of the Mass. The Eucharist embodies the significance, purpose, and goal of all priesthood in the Church. Even matrimony, as St. Thomas says, points to the Eucharist; for marriage shows forth the unity of Christ with the Church, and the Eucharist symbolizes this unity also.

The Eucharist belongs directly to the Mass, it *is* indeed the very Mass itself. In the Mass Jesus Christ becomes really present, in order that His Sacrifice on the Cross, by which He has earned new life for man, may be offered again and again in the midst of His Church. The Mass is not just a commemorative celebration; nor is it merely a communal preparation for Holy Communion. The Mass is essentially a public sacrifice; and the reception of the Body of our Lord is essentially a sacrificial act, a sacrificial meal. Christ Himself offers Himself to His Father as sacrifice for sinful mankind; and the Christian community likewise offers itself together with Christ in the same sacrifice to the Father. The priest is the instrument of the self-offering Christ, and at the same time he is the representative of the co-offering community, or congregation. By this continuing renewal of the Sacrifice of the Cross, its fruits are given to all who assist in offering the Mass. The Council of Trent says that "in order to effect our eternal salvation, Christ willed to sacrifice Himself *once* to the Father upon the altar of the Cross. But His priesthood was not to cease at His death. Therefore at the Last Supper He offered His Body and Blood to the Father in the form of bread and wine, thus bequeathing to His Church a Sacrifice through which the Sacrifice of the Cross, once offered, is made present, its memory preserved until the end of the world, and His healing power applied to us for remission of the sins which we daily commit." Every Christian should bear this meaning of the Mass in mind. The most excellent way for him to do so is to offer the Mass together with the priest.

The Mass is the public and common Sacrifice offered by the People of God. The Church strictly obliges all the faithful to assist at its public celebration every Sunday of the year and on all great feasts.

The Sacrament of Penance

The Christian is brought to new life, matured, and nourished by the sacraments of baptism, confirmation, and Holy Eucharist; but his new life remains in constant danger, either from the human will's inclination to evil, or from the "prince of this world," Satan. The life of the soul may be weakened, and even lost. But the grace of Christ, the fullness of what He earned by suffering, is sufficiently ample to heal and restore the life of the soul to full health, provided certain conditions are fulfilled. The sacrament of healing and recovery from sin is the sacrament of penance.

Man's life is properly ordered when it is directed toward man's true end—God, as revealed to us in Christ. In order to live a life directed toward this end, we must know how to evaluate all other human aims and goods at their true worth. Whoever does not know the final reason for man's existence cannot know the true value of created things for man. Man's proper relation to God, to the world, and to his fellow man is confused and destroyed by sin. Sin is man's willful straying from his true end. It is through this deeply mysterious and incomprehensible willful straying from God that all other relationships between man and the world and man and his fellow man fall into disorder. Crippled by sin, man does not live to his full capacity. He loses the fullness of his destined life —his life in God, his life of divine sonship.

Serious or grave sin, that is, conscious and complete straying of the human will from man's last end, God, is deadly in its effects and is therefore called mortal sin; for it deals death to man's new life. What is called "venial sin" does not, it is true, permanently deflect man from his last end, but it puts an obstacle in his way. The cure of the mortal illness of sin through the sacrament of penance must come both from within and from without. St. Thomas compares the process to the cure of bodily ills, where the inner healing force of nature must combine with the skill of the physician and the work of medication. The inward conquest of sin consists in not willing it any more, and in willing its opposite. The road to this conquest lies through *repentance* and *resolution*.

Repentance says *no* to sin and *yes* to good. In repentance, man takes sides with God against his own selfishness, which in turn means that he is taking sides with himself—his true self. A repentant man detests the deed he repents of, and wishes it undone. Resolution is closely linked to repentance. It is the resolve to improve and not to sin again. Unless the repentance is real, no resolution develops; and from the resolution one can tell whether or not the rejection of sin is genuine. When sin is rejected from supernatural love for God, repentance is so powerful that the sin upon the soul is erased. This is called "perfect" contrition. However, even when contrition is perfect, the obligation still remains of confessing the sin.

The cure "from without" is effected by Christ, the source and very essence of the new life and thus the originator of its restoration. When the Christian presents himself to Christ the Saviour, he is offering himself at the same time to Christ the Judge. This he does by explicitly confessing the sins he has committed; for this reason the common name for the sacrament of penance is "confession," though the actual confession is only a part of the sacrament. The priest represents the judging and saving Christ to whose judgment and saving sentence the Christian submits himself. Through the priest, His instrument, Christ our Lord remits the sins of the repentant sinner and restores him to health in the new life of the Holy Spirit. The priest's words of absolution completing the sacrament of penance are: "I absolve thee from all thy sins in the name of the Father, and of the Son, and of the Holy Ghost. Amen."

The Sacrament of Extreme Unction

Extreme unction, or last anointing, is the sacrament of those who are physically ill. Often enough it brings about physical recovery as well, but its real virtue consists in preparing a Christian to enter the glory of heaven. It takes away what might be called the remnants of sin—perverse habits, wrong inclinations, inordinate attachments, and so on—and it also remits all temporal punishment for sin. Normally, extreme unction is preceded by the sacrament of penance, but if the condition of the patient is such that this is no longer possible, then the sacrament of extreme unction itself remits even a mortal sin—provided the sinner has at least relinquished all inner attachment to his evil deed. Through this sacrament the new life in a Christian is so thoroughly restored that the soul is ready to pass over into eternal life.

As the priest anoints with holy oil the eyes, ears, nose,

mouth, hands, and feet of the patient, he says: "Through this holy anointing and through His tender mercy may the Lord forgive thee whatever sins thou hast committed by the sense of sight, by the sense of hearing, by the sense of smell, by the sense of taste and the power of speech, by the sense of touch, by the power of walking. Amen."[1]

In emergencies, the priest uses an abbreviated form. He anoints the forehead of the dying, and says: "May the Lord through this holy anointing forgive thee whatever sins thou hast committed."

The Sacrament of Holy Orders

In Christ the invisible Godhead became visible Man. The dispensers of Christ's divine life to men are themselves also visible men. The supernatural strength which nourishes this dispensing power is transferred to them from Christ by the sacrament of holy orders. The share which bishops and priests have in the divine life of Christ is thus a special share in Christ's own Priesthood, His own mediatorship between God and man. Just as we all receive the mark of a Christian in baptism, and the mark of a soldier of Christ in confirmation, so in the sacrament of holy orders a man receives the indelible mark of the Christian priesthood. Neither sin nor unworthiness on the part of the priest can diminish—let alone destroy—the priestly power thus conferred; for a priest dispenses the sacraments, not because he is a good man, but because he has received from Christ, in the sacrament of holy orders, the power to do so. This power exceeds all human ability. When he dispenses the sacraments, the priest acts neither of his own strength nor in his own name, but in the

[1] In actual practice, the whole sentence is repeated each of the six times, mentioning one sense at a time.—Tr.

strength and name of Christ as Christ's living instrument.

Priestly celibacy does not imply that marriage is unworthy of the priesthood. The priest voluntarily renounces marriage knowing that he is giving up a vital good of great worth. The purpose of his renunciation is simply and solely greater availability and freedom in the service of God.

To the bishop belong the full functions of the priesthood, and therefore only he can confer the sacrament of holy orders. He lays both his hands on the head of each candidate and after that he prays: "Hear us, we beseech Thee, Lord our God, and pour out upon these Thy servants the blessing of the Holy Spirit and the power of priestly grace. Sustain them forever with the bounty of Thy gifts, whom we present to Thy mercy to be consecrated. Through our Lord Jesus Christ, Thy Son, who lives and reigns with Thee in the unity of the same Holy Spirit, God, for ever and ever. Amen."

As the sacred ceremony of ordination continues, the bishop hands to each of the candidates the chalice containing wine and water, and the paten with a host lying on it, saying to each one as he does so: "Receive the power to offer sacrifice to God and to celebrate Mass for the living as well as for the dead. In the name of the Lord." The ordained answers "Amen."

From these words it is plain that the main priestly function and power is that of effecting the presence of the Body of our Lord at Mass, and of offering IT for sacrifice.

There are other powers, too, which the priest also receives at his ordination. The first function of the priesthood consists in the administration of the sacraments—especially, as we have seen, in performing in the name of Christ and as His instrument the transubstantiation of bread and wine into the Body and Blood of our Lord, and preparing the faithful, through the remittance of sins in the Holy Spirit, to receive the Lord's Body in Communion. The second function of the priesthood is the proper guidance of the People of God and the preservation of their unity.

In their power to offer sacrifice, all priests and bishops including the Pope are equal. But the power of ruling and guiding the People of God—the power of jurisdiction—has different degrees and levels of rank and subordination, according to the different subordinate units which go to make up the whole Church. The *pastor,* together with his priestly assistants and acting under the authority of the bishop, administers the *parish,* which is the smallest vital unit. The *bishops,* as successors to the Apostles, govern the larger unit, the *diocese.* And just as in each diocese there can be but one ruler, the bishop, so over the whole People of God, the one Catholic and Apostolic *Church,* there can be but one ruler, the *Pope.* The Pope is the successor of St. Peter, the Apostle whom our Lord appointed to be His governing representative, or vicar. The Pope is that Vicar of Christ in whom all ruling power in the Church is founded, and in whom rests the infallible custody of the deposit of faith. To protect the unity of faith and to preserve the peace of the People of God—that is the office of the Pope.

All sacramental life in the Church goes back to the bishops, the successors of the Apostles. The office of bishop includes all other priestly offices. All functions of the priesthood are exercised by the bishop, and from this fullness of priestly power flows the whole sacramental life of the diocese. As we have seen, he alone has the right to ordain priests. He alone has the right to administer confirmation, to mark the faithful with the seal of the mature soldier of Christ; he consecrates the churches and altars where the Holy Sacrifice is offered, and the chalice which the priest uses at Mass. And when the priest administers the sacrament of last anointing to the dying, he anoints them with the holy oil consecrated by the bishop on Holy Thursday.

The consecration of a bishop is performed by another bishop and two bishops attending him. It is the most solemn of all consecrations. As in ordination to the priesthood, here too the heart of the action is the laying on of hands, accompanied by special words of blessing. This ancient gesture of conferring power goes back through the ages to Christ and the Apostles.

The Sacrament of Matrimony

The continued existence of a people is assured by its constant renewal through new generations. The people of God, the Church, must likewise rely on this natural process of self-perpetuation; the source of the new generations is the family, man and woman united for life.

The family is the living cell both of civil society and of the Church, and for this reason enjoys an exalted standing both politically and ecclesiastically. Hence the high sacramental dignity of marriage and the importance of marriage laws both civil and ecclesiastical.

Jesus Christ raised the lifelong union of husband and wife to a sacrament—which is to say that He made it a source of supernatural life. To husband and wife the sacrament of matrimony affords a constant increase of new life and a protection against the dangers of concupiscence. The sacrament of matrimony confers on man and woman the strength to turn to the world and the senses in such a manner that they will not become separated from Christ and His Church; it enables them to enjoy temporal goods without losing the eternal ones.

Christian marriage has a threefold function. First, it brings forth new generations of the People of God. Second, it is the perfect bond of friendship and community of life for man and woman, established and assured by marital fidelity. Pius XI said that "this mutual inward moulding of husband and wife, this determined effort to perfect each other, can in a very real sense, as the Roman Catechism teaches, be said to be the chief reason and purpose of matrimony."[1] Third, Christian marriage symbolizes the indissoluble living bond between Christ and His Church. "You who are husbands," says St. Paul (Ephesians 5:25), "must shew love to your wives, as Christ shewed love to the Church when he gave himself up on its behalf."

Husband and wife themselves are the ones who administer the sacrament of matrimony. This they do by giving their mutual pledge in the presence of the bishop or pastor and of two additional witnesses.

The Sacraments, Fruit of the Incarnation

All the sacraments go back in their institution to Jesus Christ; for He, as "God become visible," is the Sacrament of sacraments. The sacraments derive their sanctifying power from His Incarnation and from His redeeming Passion. They are Jesus Christ's legacy to the Church, whose highest office it is to put the grace of God within the reach of all men, and to communicate it to them, especially in the public celebration of the Holy Sacrifice of the Mass.

[1] Encyclical (*Casti Connubii*) on Christian Marriage, 1930. Paulist Press pamphlet translation, New York 1941, para. 24.

We have seen that a Christian's share in the life of the Church means first of all his active participation in the sacramental life, primarily in the Holy Eucharist—in Mass and Holy Communion. But besides this it also means living the Church year. The liturgical year is made up of two different but complementary elements which dovetail. One is the week. The other is the series of feasts of Christ. In these latter the Church solemnly commemorates the separate steps of our Redemption, instituted in our Lord's Incarnation and finally wrought in His Passion and Resurrection.

The seven-day week symbolizes God's work of Creation, which Sacred Scripture divides into six days and a day of rest. Sunday, the day of the Blessed Trinity, begins the week; it commemorates the first day of Creation, the Resurrection of Jesus Christ from the dead, and the descent of the Holy Spirit on the first Pentecost. Christian piety has assigned special significance to other days of the week as well—the Passion to Friday, hence a day of abstinence in memory of our Lord's sufferings; the veneration of Mary, the Mother of God, to Saturday.

The annual cycle of the feasts of our Lord puts into tangible terms of space and time the recital of the second part of the Creed—"conceived by the Holy Ghost, born of the Virgin Mary, suffered under Pontius Pilate, was crucified, died, and was buried; he descended into hell; the third day he rose again from the dead; he ascended into heaven, sitteth at the right hand of God the Father almighty." These mysteries of our faith, by which the redemption of mankind was effected, are the subject of commemorative feasts, which follow the sequence of the Creed's recital.

Advent is the season of promise and expectation. During Advent, the Church recites in her Divine Office (or Breviary) this prayer: "We are waiting patiently and longingly for the Saviour, the Lord Jesus Christ. He will renew our poor bodies and form them into the likeness of the Body of His radiance. Let us live piously and justly in this world according to His law, persevering in blessed hope and expecting the arrival of our great and glorious God."

Christmas is the feast of the most fundamental mystery of all, the Incarnation: God, becoming flesh, is born of the Virgin Mary. "Today," sings the Divine Office, "the King of heaven deigns to be born to us of the Virgin, coming to call man back to the heavenly home he had lost. The angelic hosts are all rejoicing, because eternal salvation is now shown forth to all mankind. Glory be to God in the highest, and on earth peace to men of good will."

Lent is the season of preparation for the death and Resurrection of our Lord, the mysteries in which the salvation is finally wrought for us which the Incarnation had begun. The Christian prepares himself for these solemnities by an earnest renewal of his life through prayerful recollection, fasting, and penance.

With *Easter* we enter upon the fulfillment of our salvation in the glorious Resurrection of our Lord:

> In this great triumph death and life
> Together met in wondrous strife;
> The Prince of Life, once dead, doth reign.[1]

[1] Sequence from the Mass for Easter. Eng. tr. taken from the edition of the *Roman Missal* by Abbot Cabrol, O.S.B., New York (Kenedy) 1934.

The crowning of the Resurrection is Christ's *Ascension* into heaven, followed by His sending the Holy Spirit on *Pentecost* (or *Whitsunday*). In Matins for the Thursday of Pentecost Week, the Church sings: "The divine flame came, not burning but enlightening, not consuming but giving light. It found its way to the disciples' hearts, pure as they were to receive it, and gave them the gifts of the powers of grace. Coming upon the disciples united in love, it rushed in upon them and suffused them with the radiant grace of the Godhead."

The time from Pentecost to the following Advent is consecrated to Christ the King, enthroned at the right hand of God. The liturgy of this season develops the basic ideas of God's Kingdom among men.

The liturgical year is interwoven with a great number of feasts of the Blessed Virgin and of the saints. Its prime significance, however,—and Pope Pius X re-emphasized this—is the commemoration of the life of Jesus Christ. But the liturgical year is much more than a commemoration of the historical life of Christ in Palestine. For Christ continues to live in the Church, and the annual round of His great feasts keeps before our eyes the mysteries of Christ's life that go beyond historical reality.

Pius X reasserted that life with the Church is realized primarily by taking part in her sacramental life and in the ceremonies of her calendar. "The faithful," he said, "must draw the truly Christian spirit from its first source by taking active part in the supremely holy mysteries of the Church, and in her public and solemn prayer."

THE CHRISTIAN VIRTUES

What is Virtue

The fact that the word *virtue* has in our time taken on the tinge of something unmanly and even ridiculous imposes two obligations upon the Christian. He must beware of any falsely pious abuse of the word and concept, and he must come to recognize its healthy and genuine sense, which it is his duty to embody, regardless of any human respect.

The Latin word *virtus* means *manliness*. The German word for virtue, *Tugend*, comes from *taugen, to be fit;* and related to this is the English word *doughty*, now obsolete except in humor, but originally meaning *able*. Virtue makes a man *fit and able* to be what his Creator intends, and to do what his Creator wills.

Thus virtue is not good surface behavior and orderly deportment. A good man is more of a man than a bad one, in the sense that he is making more of his humanity. He is in every respect *more fit*. Thus a man's virtue shows that he is putting his ability into practice; here and now he is making actual what would otherwise remain merely possible within him. This means that he does good—and that he does it not because he has to, but because he wills to. He wants to, and he can. Through sin, the willful turning away from God, a man of his own free will becomes *unfit* to be and do what he is intended to be and do.

The highest and truest fitness of the Christian is to be able to lead the life of a child of God, in close relationship with God, by the power of the Holy Spirit. His most abysmal unfitness consists in losing this power and this life through his own fault.

The most important Christian virtues are the three theological virtues of faith, hope, and charity, and the four cardinal virtues of wisdom, justice, fortitude, and moderation.

The Three Theological Virtues

Faith, hope, and charity relate directly to God. Hence they are called "theological." They are man's response to the reality of the Trinity—not a reaction of the mind only, but a living response involving his whole being. They are a response which no one can give without the aid of grace; for only to the man who has received grace has the reality of the Trinity been revealed. Thus these three virtues are the fruits and effects of sanctifying grace. They make man fit for an effectiveness to which of himself he would never attain; they elevate him to a perfect and complete life otherwise beyond the reach of his own powers.

The Virtue of Faith

The first and the fundamental theological virtue is faith. First and foremost, the Christian is a believer. That means that he is convinced of the existence and the works of the Blessed Trinity. The Christian has fully realized this reality and answers God's revelation and gift of Himself with an unqualified and completely confident acceptance. The Christian is conscious of this newly experienced reality of God with the same certainty and directness as of his natural surroundings. Though he can neither see nor prove it, he is certain of it because God Himself revealed it, disclosing it to human sight in His incarnate Son, Jesus Christ, and because, by grace, he bears within himself the witness to God.

Although faith is never unreasonable, it comprises a certain element of daring. The strength to undertake the required act of daring has its source in the grace of God and in the will of man to cooperate. Man's will has the confidence to cooperate with God, because it relies upon the word of God. God is thus both the content of faith and its motive. We believe in God, and we believe God.

Christian faith includes not only an inner conviction but also an outward profession. The two go hand in hand. "Thou canst find salvation," says St. Paul (Romans 10:9-10), "if thou wilt use thy lips to confess that Jesus is the Lord, and thy heart to believe that God has raised him up from the dead. The heart has only to believe, if we are to be justified; the lips have only to make confession, if we are to be saved."

This does not mean that a Christian is in duty bound to proclaim aloud everywhere and at all times his belief in the Triune God and His works. But it most certainly does mean that he may neither conceal nor deny his faith when the glory of God and of His Church, or the salvation of his neighbor, requires him to profess it.

In the first chapter of this book we spoke in detail of the *content* of Christian faith as consisting of the reality of the Trinity and the threefold work of Creation, Redemption, and Sanctification.

The Virtue of Hope

The Christian is a man who says to himself, "Things will turn out well with me in the end." That is, he lives in hope. He who does not hope is no true Christian. The true Christian hopes for a happy end—eternal life, life in God. Eternal life is the final and real object of the virtue of hope.

This hope—the reliance on God's power and veracity—cannot be shattered by anything. "Even if he slays me," said Job (13:15), "I will hope in him." And the Christian makes these words his own.

Hope, like faith, is a gift of God, a gift that confers an indestructible youthfulness. The actual secret of "eternal youth" lies in the supernatural virtue of hope; for the hopeful Christian always knows that he is headed for the happy end infinitely surpassing all expectation—eternal life. This expectation keeps him alert and resilient. In the Book of the Prophet Isaias (40:30-31) we read: "Youths shall faint and labour: and young men shall fall by infirmity. But they that hope in the Lord shall renew their strength. They shall take wings as eagles; they shall run and not be weary; they shall walk and not faint."

Now it is true that this expectation of eternal life never leaves a Christian any rest. As long as he has not reached eternal life or become worthy of it he can never be completely satisfied with himself. As St. Augustine said, "Our hearts are restless until they rest in Thee."

But this restlessness has nothing in common with the torturing unrest of boredom and despair. It is the joyful activity of youth, happy in the knowledge that the real goal still lies ahead. And as long as a Christian is alive on this earth his goal in very truth still lies ahead of him. He will reach it in eternal life.

Yet Christian hope is not the same as final certitude. No one is definitely certain of not losing eternal life through his own fault. This is a great mystery. Man's free will and God's infallible grace cooperate in a way beyond our understanding. In our hope we know two things: that our true goal still lies ahead of us, and that we may miss it. Hence Christian hope always involves the "fear of the Lord." This is the fear of being separated from the author and essence of eternal life, God, through one's own fault.

Hope is essential to prayer. He who has ceased to hope cannot pray; and he who supposes himself already in possession of everything will not pray. But he who really hopes prays from the deepest motivation within him; for prayer is nothing else than hope expressed. St. Thomas says that *the* expression of Christian hope is the Lord's Prayer. "This, then," said our Lord (Matthew 6:9), "is to be your prayer:

"Our Father, who art in heaven, hallowed be thy name.

"Thy kingdom come.

"Thy will be done, on earth as it is in heaven.

"Give us this day our daily bread.

"And forgive us our trespasses, as we forgive them that trespass against us.

"And lead us not into temptation, but deliver us from evil."

In this prayer, St. Thomas says, everything is set forth which the Christian hopes to attain, as well as everything which he hopes to avoid. Specifically:

Eternal life (Thy kingdom come).

Fulfillment of the will of God (Thy will be done, on earth as it is in heaven).

Possession of the necessary goods of life (Give us this day our daily bread).

Forgiveness of sins (And forgive us our trespasses).

Victory over temptation (And lead us not into temptation).

Release from all distress (but deliver us from evil).

The Virtue of Charity

The greatest of all Christian virtues is the love of God and neighbor, or charity. "I may speak," wrote St. Paul in his first Epistle to the Corinthians (13:1), "with every tongue that men and angels use; yet, if I lack charity, I am no better than echoing bronze, or the clash of cymbals." And Christ said (Mark 12:28-32) that the commandments to love God and to love our neighbor were the greatest commandments there are. "One of the scribes . . . came up and asked him, Which is the first commandment of all? Jesus answered him, the First commandment of all is, Listen, Israel; there is no God but the Lord thy God; and thou shalt love the Lord thy God with the love of thy whole heart, and thy whole soul, and thy whole mind, and thy whole strength. This is the first commandment, and the Second, its like, is this, Thou shalt love thy neighbour as thyself. There is no other commandment greater than these."

Supernatural love of God and neighbor is not primarily a matter of feeling, nor is it a wallowing in sentiment. This greatest of all loves, charity, is a matter of the free decision of a man's will, enlightened by his intellect and by faith; it is the true fruit of the new life flowing into him from the Holy Spirit.

There are no bounds to the love which God deserves. This we know from our faith, especially from faith in our Redemption through Jesus Christ. How can I, a finite human being, love the infinitely lovable God as He deserves? Only by charity.

My neighbor is a child of God. This too we know from our faith. All the redeemed are "sons and heirs of God." The love of God and the love of our neighbor belong together.

In the life of the early Church the intimate connection between love of God and love of neighbor was open for all to see: the works of charity were directly and visibly combined with the sacramental meal. Everybody could notice that all Christian love of neighbor takes its origin and strength from the intimate union of God and man. On the natural level, I can love my neighbor as a friend, as my partner in marriage, as my child, my parent, my fellow-countryman. But I can love him also because God loves him so greatly that for his sake as well as for mine He sent His only-begotten Son into the world to be sacrificed. This love surpasses all purely natural love—not in emotional fervor, but in the strength of its affirmative power. Such loves does not live on human strength alone, but on the power of the Holy Spirit, by whom—as the Bible tells us (Romans 5:5)—"the love of God has been poured out in our hearts."

Supernatural Christian love participates in the love by which God loves His Son and us. And the natural love of friendship, of conjugal life, of any human association at all, receives from this supernatural love a wholly new fervor and a greatly increased strength and depth.

Supernatural love of neighbor manifests itself above all in compassion. Christian charity is ready with sympathy and instant generosity of heart to help any one in distress, whether he be friend, stranger, or enemy. Christ Himself, Incarnate God, takes the place of the one in distress; and love of God and love of neighbor thus merge into one and the same charity—because their common source is Christ. At the end of the world, Christ the Judge will say to the elect (Mt. 25:35-46): "I was hungry, and you gave me food, thirsty, and you gave me drink; I was a stranger, and you brought me home, naked, and you clothed me, sick, and you cared for me, a prisoner, and you came to me. . . . Believe me, when you did it to one of the least of my brethren here, you did it to me." And to the accursed the Judge will say: "I was hungry, and you never gave me food, I was thirsty, and you never gave me drink; I was a stranger, and you did not bring me home, I was naked, and you did not clothe me, I was sick and in prison, and you did not care for me. . . . Believe me, when you refused it to one of the least of my brethren here, you refused it to me."

Charity is the greatest of all the Christian virtues. By charity man becomes worthy of the Kingdom of God. Charity wipes out all sins; it cannot bear to be separated from God; supernatural love and sin are mutually exclusive. An act of supernatural love may suffice to justify man before God. "Make charity your aim" we are exhorted by St. Paul (Corinthians 14:1), who, in the thirteenth chapter of his first Epistle to the Corinthians, has left us the greatest hymn to charity.

The Theological Virtues and Sanctifying Grace

All three theological virtues have their roots in sanctifying grace. Their seeds are implanted in us together with grace as new potentialities which would otherwise be beyond our reach. In the order of their nature, faith comes before hope, hope before charity. And sin destroys them in reverse order—charity first, faith last. The faith of a man living in mortal sin is indeed incomplete, but it is the spark from which the flame of his supernatural life can be lit again to become full, warm, and bright.

The Four Cardinal Virtues

The cardinal virtues are natural perfections—human potentialities on the natural level. But as Christian virtues they have their roots in the supernatural soil of faith, hope, and charity; above all, in sanctifying grace. In a Christian, the infused moral virtues of prudence, justice, fortitude and temperance go far beyond their natural strength and nobility, to the fullness of the sanctity of a life centered in God.

The Virtue of Prudence

The first of the four cardinal virtues, and the rule for the other three, is prudence. Now it goes against the grain of present-day thinking to see in prudence a virtue, let alone the first of the four cardinal virtues. The reason for this is that we often have an entirely wrong idea of the virtue of prudence. Prudence as virtue has nothing to do with smartness and guile, nor with the timorous attitude of undue caution. Prudence is the quality of clearsightedness. The prudent man approaches each decision with his eyes open, in the full light of knowledge and faith. He discerns reality objectively, sizes up a factual situation for what it is, and weighs the real value of things. Only after careful consideration does the prudent man make his decision. Whoever follows the impulse of his will before appraising the facts and the circumstances of a situation accurately and objectively is imprudent and unwise. That man is prudent who directs the choice of his will according to his insight in a situation and in the true reality of things as God has created them, and who is able to apply the general principles of virtuous action to the concrete, immediate instance.

If the prudent man feels that a situation is beyond his own powers of insight, he will rely on the insight of a more competent person. Hence, docility is a part of prudence—the ability to accept instruction and advice. Presumptuousness and lack of objective reflection are the contrary of prudence. The know-it-all and the man lacking objectivity are not humble enough to match their judgment with reality. This type of person believes that he can come to a decision impetuously and blindly. However, any decision not arrived at from a sober appraisal of reality is bound to be wrong. And if such a decision concerns a matter of morals, it cannot possibly be a good one.

The person who lacks objectivity and who is unable to keep still and to allow the facts to speak, in order to gain a sound basis for his decisions, cannot possibly be a just man either. Justice and all the other cardinal virtues demand capacity for weighing facts, respect for objective reality, and ability to transform this theoretical knowledge into effective action. From all this it becomes obvious that prudence is a first requirement for the other virtues. And that is why St. Thomas calls it their "mother."

Prudence is the art of deciding wisely. The prudent man acknowledges the obligations contained in objective reality. Not only does he know what is right, he also does what he has realized to be right. The decisions based on prudence, therefore, are the verdict of our conscience. Conscientiousness and prudence are as closely related as effect and cause. Whoever works on the development of prudence in others and in himself also improves and perfects his conscience.

The Virtue of Justice

While prudence is the cornerstone of the cardinal virtues, justice is their peak and culmination. A good man is above all a just man. But what is justice? As a virtue, it makes man eminently fitted for life in common with others. Only a just man can truly live with others. The just man gives to each his due. He takes an objective and unprejudiced view in his judgments of others and of their accomplishments. He is fair. He is appreciative where appreciation is due, and his appreciation is not restricted to words but shows in his spirit and action. The just man finds his appropriate place in society, whether in the family, the community, the state and the Church. This means that a just man is disciplined and knows how to obey and how to command, how to praise and how to blame, all with incorruptible objectivity, whether his position be that of a leader or subordinate. He never talks behind another's back, nor does he pass on to others whatever evil he may hear of his fellow man. He does not even listen to it. The Bible admonishes us to frown on the slanderer: "The north wind stops rain, and a frown a backbiter" (Proverbs 25:23).

Also opposed to justice is the hasty and ill-considered fault-finding with the orders of legitimate authority. The just man is fair here too. He is neither petty nor ungracious nor self-righteous.

Above all else, the just man is truthful. Truthfulness is one of the cornerstones of communal life. Wherever truth ceases to be respected, communal life breaks up and falls apart, whether within the family, among friends, or in the greater social bodies of nation and world. The virtue of justice alone makes men fit to live together in true peace and genuine harmony.

Whenever Sacred Scripture wants to single out someone as particularly perfect—St. Joseph, for example, the foster father of our Lord—it calls him "a just man" (Matthew 1:19). "Treasures of wickedness shall profit nothing: but justice shall deliver from death" (Proverbs 10:2).

The Virtue of Fortitude

Good does not prevail of itself. Courageous men have to stand up for it. It is one of the basic errors of liberalism to suppose that good will prevail without the support of ready courage, or fortitude. The consequences of the virtue of fortitude consist essentially and precisely in the readiness to fight for the cause of good in the world and to set one's defenses against the powers of evil.

The courageous man is ready to suffer injuries in this battle, and by that we mean anything disagreeable to human nature, such as misunderstanding, scorn, ridicule, as well as harm to his body and his possessions. In this battle, the man of courage is even willing to give his life. Death in a good cause is the noblest show of fortitude, and the readiness to die is its very essence.

The greatest cause a man can stand up for is the cause of Jesus Christ. Martyrdom for Christ is therefore the highest achievement Christian fortitude can reach. Its close second is death for the community, particularly death in a just war for the rights and peace of one's people.

Now fortitude, in order to be virtuous, must be linked to justice. Only the just man can be truly courageous, and true fortitude is to be found only if the fight is for a just cause. The courage of the criminal is not fortitude. Hence St. Thomas Aquinas says that "the praise of fortitude depends upon justice"; and St. Ambrose, that "courage without justice is a prying tool of the evil one."

Courage, however, is shown not in attack only, but also in endurance. As every seasoned soldier knows, it may be a much braver thing to hold one's ground than to attack. To storm an enemy position calls for less moral fortitude than to sit out a heavy bombardment. The same is true of martyrdom, the crown of Christian fortitude. We may well say that martyrdom consists in holding one's ground and enduring for the cause of Christ.

Patience is a part of fortitude; patience, in the Christian sense, means firmness of soul that does not weaken under the constant attack of sorrow nor in the face of cruelty and evil. However, the readiness of the courageous Christian to endure patiently even unto death does not imply that he will refrain altogether from attack. His courage in attack will gain from his patient endurance; for this gives him a detachment and freedom of mind denied to mere "men of action" who despise patience as an "unmanly" quality.

The Virtue of Moderation, or Temperance

Since the fall of Adam we have not been able to take an ordered inner life for granted. We are faced with the constant possibility of the revolt of the senses against the spirit. The desire for sensual enjoyment, whether it be in eating, in drinking, or in sexual intercourse, may exceed the measure set by God and by reason. And the immoderation of such desire destroys man's interior order. The essence of the cardinal virtue of moderation, traditionally called temperance, consists in not allowing one's will for enjoyment to exceed due measure. The human will for enjoyment may easily reach destructive proportions, but not in the temperate man.

Sins against this virtue in eating and drinking and sexual life differ from offenses against the other virtues in that they plainly bear the mark of disgrace and shame. All intemperance, especially incontinence, runs directly counter to man's true dignity and worth as a rational spiritual being. A man who cannot control his desire sinks below the level of an animal. He grows more and more apart from one of the greatest goods ever given to him, his inner freedom of choice. Only the disciplined man can make clear and calm and free decisions. In the words of St. Thomas, intemperance is slavery. Its victim eventually grows dull to all spiritual values and unreceptive to divine things. Whereas temperance, restraint, and chastity are signs of manliness and maturity, immoderation of whatever kind is a sign of immaturity. Therefore a Christian, for the sake of higher spiritual and divine goods, will keep his desires in check even when they are not directed to evil. The Preface of the Mass in Lent gives thanks to God for this restraint, "for by this bodily fasting thou dost curb vice and uplift the mind, bestowing upon us virtue and its rewards, through Christ our Lord."

Now as we have seen, temperance is not the greatest of the cardinal virtues. The greatest is justice, the virtue of community life. But he who cannot be temperate cannot be just either. So while we must not make the mistake of supposing temperance, abstemiousness, and chastity to be the only virtues of a Christian, or even his highest or most important ones, neither must we forget that without these virtues no full and perfect life is possible. We must also bear in mind that the world of today has little respect for restraint and chastity, and that these virtues are therefore in particular danger. It is therefore important that these virtues be understood in their true nature, without any distortion or exaggeration. They are the virtues of manliness and moral cleanliness, of human dignity and of honor, and of that inner freedom which comes with clear-headed and disciplined maturity.

The Ten Commandments

In the sevenfold picture of the three theological and the four cardinal virtues we have given an outline of the Christian image of the good man. It is by these virtues that the Christian is enabled to live in accordance with the commandments of God.

God gave the Ten Commandments to the people among whom He was one day to raise the Messias. We know from St. Paul's Epistle to the Romans (2:15) that the commandments of God were also engraved in the hearts of the heathen. They are the "Law" which Christ said He had not come to destroy but to fulfill. In the Sermon on the Mount (Matthew 5,6,7) He says: "You have heard that it was said to the men of old, Thou shalt do no murder; if a man commits murder, he must answer for it before the court of justice. But I tell you that any man who is angry with his brother must answer for it before the court of justice" (Matthew 5:21f).

This comparison between the Old and the New Law—"You have heard that it was said to the men of old . . . But I tell you . . ."—is repeated many times; it shows that the life of a Christian is measured by a higher standard, and a stricter one, than the life of either pre-Christian man or pagan man.

The Ten Commandments are:

I am the Lord thy God;

1. Thou shalt not have strange gods before me;
2. Thou shalt not take the name of the Lord thy God in vain;
3. Remember that thou keep holy the Sabbath day;
4. Honor thy father and thy mother;
5. Thou shalt not kill;
6. Thou shalt not commit adultery;
7. Thou shalt not steal;
8. Thou shalt not bear false witness against thy neighbor;
9. Thou shalt not covet thy neighbor's wife;
10. Thou shalt not covet thy neighbor's goods.

It is important to bear in mind that these commandments were given, not to an individual, but to a people—the Chosen People of God. They contain the principles of every just and healthy social order. The first three commandments indicate that proper order prevails only in a society which believes in God, fears Him, and puts the belief into practice, rendering to God the public honor which is His due as supreme King and Lord. Hence the institution of the Sabbath, or day of rest, our Sunday, the observance of which extends to civil life as well as religious. The fourth commandment declares the need to recognize legitimate authority in family, community, and state. This condition is essential if a society is to survive. In the fifth commandment God declares the life of each individual human being to be sacred and inviolable. It may not be touched by threat or injury from any unlawful or self-appointed power whatever. A society in which the life of the individual is not respected will go down in ruin. The sixth and ninth commandments protect marriage as the basis of the family and of all society. The seventh and tenth protect the right of private property. The economic and legal orders are thus given their moral and religious foundation. From the eighth commandment we learn that it is truth and truthfulness which hold society together, and that falsehood destroys it.

Belief in God, service of God, obedience to legitimate authority, respect for human life, respect for the sanctity of marriage, protection of property, perfect maintenance of truth and veracity—these are the basic prerequisites for a truly moral public order. And no one but the virtuous man is fit to fulfill them.

Christ, our Model

The whole point of a Christian's life is to become like Christ. It can be put even more strongly: the Christian is to become *another Christ*. In the words of St. Paul (Ephesians 4:13), the Christian is to "reach perfect manhood, that maturity which is proportioned to the completed growth of Christ." For Christ said, "You are to be perfect, as your heavenly Father is perfect" (Matthew 5:48).

The fullness of Christ's own Life is treasured up in the Church. The Church imparts it to her members by virtue of their life with the Church, especially in the sacraments. This life, which the Christian receives in the Church through Jesus Christ, forms him into a new man. By the power of faith, hope, and charity, he matures into a constructive and good man: prudent, just, courageous, and moderate,—able and willing to keep the commandments of God.

THE FULFILLMENT OF FAITH AND LIFE

Jesus Christ said, "The man who has faith in me enjoys eternal life" (John 6:47), and "The kingdom of heaven will not give entrance to every man who calls me Master, Master; only to the man that does the will of my Father who is in heaven" (Matthew 7:21). In heaven, Christian faith becomes Beatific Vision—seeing God face to face—and Christian life becomes the eternal life of glory.

It should hardly be necessary to remark that heaven is not some glorified juvenile playground, nor some everlasting place of sanctimonious boredom. Such concepts are childish and unworthy. The kingdom of heaven is the fulfillment of all human longing—friendship with God that cannot be lost, eternal bliss. It is of this that the mysterious revelation of St. John speaks when it says:

"Then I saw a new heaven, and a new earth. The old heaven, the old earth had vanished, and there was no more sea. And I, John, saw in my vision that holy city which is the new Jerusalem, being sent down by God from heaven, all clothed in readiness, like a bride who has adorned herself to meet her husband. I heard, too, a voice which cried aloud from the throne, Here is God's tabernacle pitched among men; he will dwell with them, and they will be his own people, and he will be among them, their own God. He will wipe away every tear from their eyes, and there will be no more death, or mourning, or cries of distress, no more sorrow; those old things have passed away. And he who sat on the throne said, Behold, I make all things new. (These words I was bidden write down, words most sure and true.) And he said to me, It is over. I am Alpha, I am Omega, the beginning of all things and their end; those who are thirsty shall drink—it is my free gift—out of the spring whose water is life. Who wins the victory? He shall have his share in this; I will be his God, and he shall be my son" (Apocalypse 21:1-7).

Two things, says the Roman Catechism, go to make up eternal life—seeing God as He is, and becoming like unto God. "For those who taste Him, although they retain their own essence, are clothed in a wonderful and well-nigh godly form, so that they are taken rather for God than for men."

SACRED SCRIPTURE

Tradition and Sacred Scripture, the Two Sources of Divine Revelation

The Christian faith as set down in the Creed (or confession of faith) rests upon the supernatural revelation of God. This means that it relies upon a direct utterance of the Divinity, God proclaiming Himself in a specific message. This message is essentially different and infinitely superior to the "natural" revelations of God which we get from all of creation, from human conscience, and from seeing the governed order of the universe. This supernatural message from God to man is the content of the Christian faith as presented by the Church in her obligatory doctrine. This supernatural revelation, our heritage of faith, is contained and set down in the oral tradition of the Church and in Sacred Scripture.

For the Church's own statement on this subject we may quote from the Vatican Council (1869-1870), which was using in part the words of the Council of Trent (1545-1563) when it said that "according to the belief of the universal Church this supernatural revelation is contained in the written books and unwritten traditions which have come down to us. These traditions were received by the Apostles either from the mouth of Christ Himself or at the dictation of the Holy Spirit, and they have been transmitted, as it were from hand to hand, even to our own day."

The main reason for calling Sacred Scripture sacred—for calling, that is to say, the Holy Bible holy—is that it is the document of God's own revelation about Himself. The Holy Ghost *inspired* it, the literal meaning of which is that He *breathed into* it. Men wrote it down, but they did so as instruments of the Holy Spirit, who, so to speak, guided their pens. What St. Peter says of the Prophets (2 Peter 1:21) applies to the Bible as a whole: "It was never man's impulse, after all, that gave us prophecy; men gave it utterance, but they were men whom God had sanctified, carried away, as they spoke, by the Holy Spirit." So Sacred Scripture is the word of God; it has, as the Vatican Council says, "God for its author"; and this is the principal reason that it is sacred.

A further reason is that by its saving teaching it leads men to holiness and to their salvation. The priest concludes the reading of the Gospel at Mass by saying, "Through the Gospel words may our sins be wiped away."

The Old and New Testaments: One Unit

Sacred Scripture consists of two parts, the Old Testament and the New Testament. The dividing line between them is also the connection between them: Jesus Christ, in whom supernatural revelation was completed. Christ is also the actual content of both Testaments. "The Old Testament comes to light in the New, the New lies hidden in the Old."

The essence of the Old Testament is Christ, the promised Redeemer, as seen in the history of the Chosen People from whom He was to come. Fundamentally, this first part of Sacred Scripture is the preparation for the salvation which Christ was to bring to man. Of the books of the Old Testament Christ Himself says: "Indeed, it is of these I speak as bearing witness to me" (John 5:39).

The New Testament deals with the historical figure of Jesus, who shows Himself to be the promised Redeemer and the eternal Son of God become Man. It describes His life, suffering, and Resurrection, as well as the teaching which He left to His Church.

Thus one can by no means separate the Old Testament from the New; for both have basically one and the same content—Christ. Christ Himself often emphasized this unbreakable bond between His own life and death and the Scriptures which they were fulfilling. St. Luke (4:16-21) has given us a sublime instance of this testimony:

"Then [Jesus] came to Nazareth, where he had been brought up; and he went into the synagogue there, as his custom was, on the sabbath day, and stood up to read. The book given to him was the book of the prophet Isaias; so he opened it, and found the place where the words ran: The Spirit of the Lord is upon me; he has anointed me, and sent me out to preach the gospel to the poor, to restore the broken-hearted; to bid the prisoners go free, and the blind have sight; to set the oppressed at liberty, to proclaim a year when men may find acceptance with the Lord. Then he shut the book, and gave it back to the attendant, and sat down. All those who were in the synagogue fixed their eyes on him, and thus he began speaking to them, This scripture which I have read in your hearing is to-day fulfilled."

The Old Testament

The Old Testament is divided into historical, prophetic, and didactic books. The Book of Genesis (Creation), also known as the first Book of Moses, is the first of the historical books and of particular importance. Its first chapter tells of the creation of the world, and its opening words are: "God, at the beginning of time, created heaven and earth." The other historical books tell mainly of the fate of the people of Israel—their selection by God, their faith in God, their hope in the Messias, and their resistances and rebellions against God's guidance.

The prophetic books are the ones which contain the most express references to Christ, the coming Saviour of the world. One of the greatest of the Prophets is Isaias, called the Evangelist among the Prophets since as mouthpiece of the Holy Spirit he gave the most ample prophecies about the Messias and foretold His Virgin Birth. It is also in the Book of Isaias that we find the cry of longing that went up from pre-Christian humanity: "Send down dew from above, you heavens, and let the skies pour down upon us the rain we long for, him, the Just One" (Isaias 45:8. Translation from the Missal, Introit for the Fourth Sunday of Advent).

Other books of the Old Testament which we should single out for mention are: The Book of Job, a heartrending testimony to man's indestructible hope in the redemption from all suffering—"Even if he slays me, I will hope in him" (Job 13:15); and the Book of Psalms, or songs of praise, a collection of magnificently simple prayers which the Church has kept singing since her earliest days in solemn choral chant. From the Psalms (Psalm 129) we have the ancient words, "Out of the depths have I cried unto thee, O Lord; Lord hear my voice." And from the Psalms too, the great song of praise (Psalm 116): "Praise the Lord, all you Gentiles, let all the nations of the world do him honour. Abundant has his mercy been towards us; the Lord remains faithful to his word for ever."

The books of the New Testament contain principally the account of the life, work, and teaching of Jesus Christ. This is true, first, of the four Gospels. The word *gospel* means *glad tidings* or *good news*. The Gospel is the good news of the arrival among us of God become Man, the good news that His Kingdom really exists, the good news of all the gifts of God imparted to man through faith in Christ and through the sacraments of His Church. In the Gospels the Church possesses unerring remembrance of the words and works of Jesus Christ. They are recorded by Matthew and John, two Apostles who accompanied our Lord everywhere He went for more than two years, and by Mark and Luke, two disciples of the Apostles.

The Gospel of Matthew makes an especially strong point of the unbreakable link between the Old and New Testaments: Jesus Christ is the King and Messias proclaimed by the prophets and expected by the Jews; He is the Anointed of God, the Saviour of His people and of all the peoples of the earth. He is the founder of the Kingdom of God and of the new and eternal covenant (agreement) between God and Man. The Kingdom of God, or Kingdom of Heaven, is fundamentally Christ Himself, who guarantees to all men a share in His own divine life. The underlying thought of the whole Gospel of Matthew is this Kingdom of God, first proclaimed to the people of Israel, then rejected by the Jews, but now actually a fact —the Church of Jesus Christ. The Apostles are to lead all peoples to the Church by teaching and baptism.

The Evangelist Mark was a follower and what we would call the secretary of St. Peter. His main concern is to give an account of the life of the Messias from His first public appearance to His Resurrection. The Gospel of

Mark is the Gospel of the power of God which overcomes everything that is against God—suffering, death and sin.

The Gospel of Luke, who says of himself that he is the travelling companion of St. Paul (Acts 16:10 ff), has been called the *evangelium gloriæ Dei,* or glad tidings of the glory of God. St. Luke writes with a powerful and picturesque style, reminiscent of St. Paul; and the content of his Gospel, too, reminds us of St. Paul; St. Paul was the Apostle to the Gentiles, and St. Luke shows with striking clarity that Christ is the Redeemer of all peoples of mankind as well as of the Jews. Just how the Kingdom of God burst the bonds of Judaism and came to the heathen peoples—this is the tremendous historical process which St. Luke describes in the Book of Acts. And in his Gospel as well, St. Luke is the writer of historical perspective; for he discloses in basic outline the history of the Church during the life of Jesus Christ on earth.

The fourth Gospel, crown and climax to the other three, stems from the pen of the Apostle John. Besides being an Apostle, St. John was the intimate friend of our Lord. He did not write his Gospel until he was near the end of his very long life. Whereas the first three Gospels are primarily factual accounts of events, the Gospel of John contains over and above this a profound exposition of our Lord's teaching. John's main purpose is to record the "words of eternal life" which the Incarnate Word of God had spoken. Whereas the first three Gospels fix their attention rather on God *Incarnate,* John fixes his on the Incarnate *God.* The Church has incorporated into the ceremony of the Mass the magnificent opening section of St. John's Gospel, so that at the end of almost every Mass the priest reads the passage which begins, "In the beginning was the Word, and the Word was with God and the Word was God."

Next in order of arrangement after the four Gospels comes the book called the Acts of the Apostles, which, as we said, St. Luke wrote in continuation of his Gospel. It begins with the Ascension of our Lord, and ends with the account of St. Paul's missionary activity in Rome. Thus it embraces the span of time from the first flowering of the Church of Jesus Christ among the Jewish people to its establishment in Rome, its new center. The Book of Acts describes the growth of Christianity to a world religion, and it shows how the promises made to Israel were transferred from the Jews to the Gentiles in order that the Kingdom of God on earth might be built up by them. Christ gave the Apostles a missionary command (Matthew 28:19): "You, therefore, must go out, making disciples of all nations, and baptizing them in the name of the Father, and of the Son, and of the Holy Ghost." The Book of Acts is the story of the first obedience to this command.

Letters written by the Apostles give further testimony to the same missionary activity, and they constitute a large part of the New Testament. They complete and continue the personal teaching and labors of the Apostles in the newly founded communities. These letters, usually called the Epistles, are by the following Apostles: fourteen by St. Paul, one by St. James, two by St. Peter, three by St. John, and one by St. Jude (also called Thaddæus).

The fourteen Epistles of St. Paul come first. St. Thomas Aquinas says that they contain almost the whole of theology. The Apostle Paul, a man of passionate practicality, vast breadth of spirit, and openness of heart, tells us himself how he came to be called to preach the Gospel. "The gospel I preached to you is not a thing of man's dictation; it was not from man that I inherited or learned it, it came to me by a revelation from Jesus Christ. You have been told how I bore myself in my Jewish days, how I persecuted God's Church beyond measure and tried to destroy it, going further in my zeal as a Jew than many of my own age and race, so fierce a champion was I of the traditions handed down by my forefathers. And then, he who had set me apart from the day of my birth, and called me by his grace, saw fit to make his Son known in me, so that I could preach his gospel among the Gentiles" (Gal. 1:11-16).

Thus did Paul become one of the greatest of Christ's Apostles. He made numerous missionary journeys—one even as far as Spain—and more than anyone else he laid the foundations for the universal Church.

Of his fourteen Epistles, that to the Romans and that to the Hebrews are especially significant. The Epistle to the Romans, to put it briefly, deals with the grace which Jesus Christ, through His Redemption, has granted to all those who believe in Him. Without this grace, no one can achieve friendship with God, whether he belongs to the chosen Jewish people or not. Through a living faith, nourished by the love of God, a man becomes a member of the Mystical Body of Christ, a "son of God," and an heir to eternal blessedness. Just as Adam brought spiritual death, or separation from God, upon us all, so Christ has become the sole author of our life in God, which is grace.

The Epistle to the Hebrews develops the teaching that Jesus Christ mediates between God and man. Christ is the High Priest who gave Himself as the new and true Sacrifice for the forgiveness of sins. The Old Covenant and its sacrifices were but foreshadowings of this New and Eternal Testament between God and man, mere figures in anticipation of the new and everlasting Self-Sacrifice of Jesus Christ now performed on our altars.

Of the remaining Apostolic letters of the New Testament, the two of St. Peter and the three of St. John are worth particular mention. In his first Epistle St. Peter reminds us what greatness and what dignity the People of God have received by being made one in Christ. "You are a chosen race," he says (and he is talking to the whole Church, not to the Jewish people), "a royal priesthood, a consecrated nation, a people God means to have for himself" (1 Peter 2:9). The second Epistle of Peter is the last will and testament of this the first Pope, who knows his martyrdom now to be near. "I am assured, by what our Lord Jesus Christ has made known to me, that I must fold my tent before long. And I will see to it that, when I am gone, you shall always be able to remember what I have been saying. We were not crediting fables of man's invention, when we preached to you about the power of our Lord Jesus Christ, and about his coming; we had been eyewitnesses of his exaltation. Such honour, such glory was bestowed on him by God the Father, that a voice came to him out of the splendour which dazzles human eyes; This, it said, is my beloved Son, in whom I am well pleased; to him, then, listen. We, his companions on the holy mountain, heard that voice coming from heaven" (2 Peter 1:14-18).

The three Epistles of St. John have one basic theme—love. "Beloved, let us love one another; love springs from God; no one can love without being born of God, and knowing God. How can the man who has no love have any knowledge of God, since God is love? What has revealed the love of God, where we are concerned, is that he has sent his only-begotten Son into the world, so that we might have life through him. That love resides, not in our shewing any love for God, but in his shewing love for us first, when he sent out his Son to be an atonement for our sins. Beloved, if God has shewn such love to us, we too must love one another. No man has ever seen God;

but if we love one another, then we have God dwelling in us, and the love of God has reached its full growth in our lives" (1 John 4:7-12).

The last book of the New Testament is a prophetic book, called the Apocalypse (which means *revelation*). It was set down by St. John the Apostle as a record of the visions he had during his exile on the island of Patmos, in the Aegean Sea. The Apocalypse gives an account of the last days of the Church Militant when, as St. Thomas graphically puts it, "she will enter the bridal chamber of Jesus Christ to begin her life of glory." Thus the Apocalypse is the Church's book of consolation on her long and painful journey through time and the world. Whereas the prophetic books of the Old Testament foretell the first coming of our Lord in His Incarnation, this prophetic book proclaims His Second Coming, when He shall judge the world and complete His Kingdom.

Sacred Scripture was written, not primarily for the individual reader, but for the People of God, the Holy Church. Sacred Scripture is the word of God, and the Church of Jesus Christ is the work and Kingdom of God. The two cannot be separated. Hence the literal or verbal content of Sacred Scripture must never be separated from God's living effectiveness in the historical life of the Church. The true meaning of Sacred Scripture becomes clear only in connection with the teaching function of the Church of Jesus Christ. She alone is able to preserve the deposit of faith which Christ gave her; she alone has the key to the understanding of Sacred Scripture, enabling her to present, explain, and defend the true meaning of the word of God, whether it be contained in Scripture or in Tradition; for she alone is "the Church of the living God, the pillar and foundation upon which the truth rests" (1 Timothy 3:15).

The true meaning of Sacred Scripture is by no means always obvious and within the easy reach of everybody. Nor do the words of Sacred Scripture always have a single meaning only. The actual significance of words and events often lies hidden behind the obvious one. God, as St. Thomas says, has the power not only to give a certain meaning to words (even we can do that) but as Creator He can elevate both things and events to become signs and symbols, so that they signify something greater than themselves. And God is the author of Sacred Scripture. We do not, therefore, always grasp the complete sense of Sacred Scripture when we understand merely the verbal meaning, although all deeper interpretation must start from the verbal sense. Finding the deeper sense in its fullness lies beyond the natural powers of the individual. Only the Church of Jesus Christ can do this, and she does it with the help of the Holy Spirit, the Spirit of Truth of whom Christ said to the Apostles that He would be with them forever.

Sacred Scripture and the Christian

Sacred Scripture, especially the New Testament, should be in the hands of every adult Christian. The author of *The Imitation of Christ* says that next to the sacramental food of the Body of our Lord, the most necessary spiritual nourishment for the soul of the Christian is the reading of Sacred Scripture. "We shall never desist," wrote Pope Benedict XV in 1920, "from urging the faithful to read the Gospels, the Acts, and the Epistles daily, so as to gather thence food for their souls."[1] Not a single Christian family, he said, should be without the New Testament.

[1] Encyclical, *Spiritus Paraclitus,* September 15, 1920.

SOME REMARKS ON CHURCH HISTORY

World History and the Gospel of the Kingdom of God

Before ascending into heaven, Jesus Christ said to His Apostles: "All authority in heaven and on earth has been given to me; you, therefore, must go out, making disciples of all nations, and baptizing them in the name of the Father, and of the Son, and of the Holy Ghost, teaching them to observe all the commandments which I have given you. And behold I am with you all through the days that are coming, until the consummation of the world" (Matthew 28:18-20). The Apostles are to "preach the gospel to the whole of creation" (Mark 16:15); "repentance and remission of sins should be preached in [Christ's] name to all nations, beginning at Jerusalem" (Luke 24:47).

This preaching of the Gospel to the heathen has been going on ever since. It will continue until the Second Coming, when Christ comes to judge. Church history reaches the whole way from the Ascension to the Last Judgment; and for all that time, however long it may be, the Church will never cease to proclaim the good news of the Kingdom of God in the name of Christ. The Kingdom of God, mystically present with us now in Christ, its keys guarded by the Church, is the hidden axis of the whole of world history.

Christ did not send the Apostles out unfortified; for He also said to them: "Behold, I am sending down upon you the gift which was promised by my Father; you must wait in the city, until you are clothed with power from on high" (Luke 24:48). So they remained in Jerusalem until the Holy Spirit came down upon them. Preaching the faith as they were bidden could not and ought not to be the work of the unaided humanity of the bearers of faith.

Christ had also fore-ordained the way the preaching of the Gospel was to take: "You are to be my witnesses in Jerusalem and throughout Judæa, in Samaria, yes, and to the ends of the earth" (Acts 1:8). So they began in Jerusalem. Thousands came to be baptized. Together with the Apostles and disciples of Jesus they formed the first Christian community. But the leaders of the Jewish people rejected the Gospel of the risen Christ. The Jews were the first people called by God to have a share in the fruit of Christ's redemptive suffering; but only a part of them was taken into the Church. When Paul and Barnabas, therefore, were preaching to the Jews at Antioch, they said: "We were bound to preach God's word to you first; but now, since you reject it, since you declare yourselves unfit for eternal life, be it so; we will turn our thoughts to the Gentiles" (Acts 13:46).

It was difficult for the Apostles to come to this decision. They were Jews themselves. True, it was the stubbornness of many of their fellow-Jews that forced them to it. Many Jews, taking an unhealthy pride in belonging to the Chosen People of God, failed to understand what the Old Testament had said about the calling of the Gentiles. In Abraham, *all* peoples had been blessed; God had called the heathen peoples to salvation too. Peter, the chief of the Apostles, the rock upon which the Church is founded—even he had to be urged by a vision to receive the first Gentile into the Church. Yet this was a Roman Captain, Cornelius, a member of the people that, after centuries of struggle, ruled the greatest empire the world had seen.

The Book of Acts, recording the first decades of the Church's life, also tells us of the calling of Paul—a Jew who was a Roman citizen. Christ, transfigured, appeared to him. Thus was Paul, the fanatical persecutor of the infant Christian community, chosen to be the Apostle to the Gentiles. It was his preaching more than anything else which spread the Gospel throughout the Roman Empire. From the witness of living Christian tradition we know too that Peter, who had received the first Roman into the Church, himself came to Rome, the capital of the world.

Rome was then the center of paganism. There all the gods were honored. In this modern "Babylon" Peter headed the Christian community, and from there he wrote his pastoral letters to the whole Church. Like Paul he gave witness to Christ in martyrdom. Here, then, after the Gospel had been preached in Jerusalem, Judæa, and Samaria, the Church had found her final center—Rome.

The Three Great Periods of Church History

Nearly two thousand years have passed since the Gospel was first preached. We know from history how the Church has striven, through all these centuries, to carry out the command of Christ to make all nations His disciples. Now in preaching the Gospel, human messengers do not rely upon themselves alone. Christ stands ever at their side.

He continues His work in the Church through the Holy Spirit.

In order to trace an outline of Church history, the many happenings in this long span of time are best divided into the successive stages of the spread of the Gospel. First comes the Christianization of the Roman empire. This is followed by the conversion of the new peoples that begin to appear in the western part of the empire and the areas beyond it, only just coming out of hitherto unexplored regions into the light of history. These peoples were beginning to form what we now call Europe. United in one and the same Christian faith and in one and the same form of worship, they constituted Western Christendom. The third period is marked by the spread of Europeans all over the world, and by the beginnings of the Christianization of non-European peoples.

In the course of three centuries the Church penetrated and spread through the great and mighty area of the Roman empire. She grew under persecution, she overcame heathen cults, and she finally established her faith as the only one officially recognized, or even tolerated, by the state. Through years of struggle she had become strong both within and without; but yet she was furrowed by the ravages of human weakness, of party strife, and of error. She saw and survived the outward and inward collapse of Rome's imperial world, an empire already in decline when the Apostles were beginning to preach the word of God.

Next, the Church carried her good news to the Germanic tribes which had overrun the Western Roman empire. She carried it even further—to the Celts and the Britons, the Danes and the Swedes, the Normans, the Wends, and the Poles—while the converted tribes of Central Europe gradually amalgamated to form the German people. Thus in the course of centuries Western Christendom took shape and became an ever more decisive force in history; it was divided into various language groups but united by the one worship in the language of Rome. This second period embraces almost ten centuries. There were many peoples, many cultures, many levels of culture; but each contributed something to the whole; and today there is hardly a European people which cannot point with pride to some accomplishment which helped build up the Christendom of the West, where Christian faith and Christian life were the soul and body and driving force of the whole social structure.

On the other hand it was in this period, too, that the Church suffered heavy losses. The Eastern Church fell away, and has led a separate existence ever since. Africa, Asia Minor, and some parts of Europe were lost to Mohammedanism. The Western peoples, it is true, undertook the Crusades to regain the Holy Land, then in the hands of the infidel. But they won no permanent victory over the doctrine which Mohammed had started in Arabia, and which the Moslems had spread from there in fanatical warfare. So this period had its persecutions too—wherever Mohammedanism penetrated into Christian territory. There were heretics and heresies; human weakness and human malice ran their course. And finally, Western Christendom itself went into a decline. The Church suffered the fateful blow delivered by the Reformation, and the peoples of the West lost the unity of faith.

In this second period, as well as later in the third, the Church continued to expand; new peoples came into its reach. In the thirteenth century, the Far East came into contact with the Western peoples and with the Church. In 1245 the Ecumenical Council of Lyons sent a legate to Genghis Khan, who ruled the vast empire covering practically the whole of Asia. In the early part of the fourteenth century a member of the Order of St. Francis of Assisi was consecrated the first Archbishop of Pekin. The great missionary command of Christ continued to be carried out.

In the centuries that followed, the Western peoples, in spite of their quarrels and divisions among themselves, managed to conquer the greater part of the remaining world. They discovered America and Australia. They greatly expanded their knowledge of Asia. They conquered whole kingdoms and empires, traded with newly discovered peoples, and ruled the seas. Their scientific and technical advances permitted them to exploit the resources of the earth and to harness the forces of nature.

Following close upon the explorers, and often accompanying them, came the missionaries of the Church. The prophecy of Isaias began to be fulfilled which had said: "Summons of thine shall go out to a nation thou never knewest; peoples that never heard of thee shall hasten to thy call; such the glory thy God, the Holy One of Israel, has bestowed on thee" (Isaias 55:5). Missionaries came to America; and in Africa, the northern part of which had once belonged to the Roman empire and had had a Christian flowering of its own, men once more preached the Gospel. Missionaries were often the first Europeans to emigrate to the newly discovered peoples, as was the case in Japan.

The special mission of this third period seems to be to carry the Gospel to the farthest reaches, to draw all peoples, without exception, within hearing distance of the glad tidings. We have reached the time when for every people the hour of decision has struck, as the Church arrives with her message. As our Lord foretold, the Apostles have now in very truth and deed reached the ends of the earth. Neither human frailty nor human wickedness, neither erring nor straying could interfere with the fulfillment of this prophecy. There is hardly a people on earth today which has not heard the news of Christ, the Son of God and Lord of all mankind.

Every people, furthermore, hears the Gospel preached in its own tongue; the miracle of the many tongues wrought on the first Pentecost is now every-day reality: every language of the world has made Christ's message its own, translated into the words peculiar to its own genius. Such is the situation in our time; and it is of the end of time that divine revelation says: "And then I saw a great multitude, past all counting, taken from all nations and tribes and peoples and languages. These stood before the throne in the Lamb's presence, clothed in white robes, with palm branches in their hands" (Apocalypse 7:9).

The Church and her Hallmarks of Eternity

Throughout all the changes of history and time, the Church preserves her everlasting nature—natural, but supernatural; historical, but above history. It is for these hallmarks of eternity that the Christian will watch particularly as he reviews and ponders the records of Church history.

In all ages up to and including the present one, the Church has steadily been, and still is, the One, Holy, Catholic, and Apostolic Church. Until the end of all history, she will remain so. The guarantee we have for the indestructible oneness and sameness of the Church is St. Peter. To him and to his successors Christ gave the promise, "Thou art Peter [i.e., the rock], and it is upon this rock that I will build my church; and the gates of hell shall not prevail against it" (Matthew 16:18).

The power of every ecclesiastical office can be traced back in an unbroken line through all the centuries to St. Peter and the other Apostles. Even as at the time of the first Christian communities, so also today, the words of Sacred Scripture apply: "All those who had taken his words to heart . . . occupied themselves continually with the apostles' teaching, their fellowship in the breaking of bread, and the fixed times of prayer" (Acts 2:41-42).

The Church the Bedrock of Truth

The Church has always considered it her most exalted office to preserve pure and unaltered the divine revelation entrusted to her. At all times she has proclaimed this revelation to the world and to Christendom. In her progress through world history, the Church has again and again given new expression to the doctrine of the Triune God and His works, unfolding with ever growing clarity the deposit of faith contained in Scripture and Tradition. Thus she protects the deposit of faith against the untiring opposition of falsehood and error. In every century of Church history, false teachers have stepped forward and taught false doctrine. But the Church has always had the strength, not only to reject what was false and thus preserve her members from heresy, but also to use the occasion to display the true faith all the more brightly against the dark background of the opposition. This she has done by choosing the very time of some prevailing heresy to form the deposit of faith into clear dogmas.

The guardian and guarantee of this purity of faith is the Pope, to whom—in the person of St. Peter— our Lord gave the gift of infallibility. Hence the much misunderstood dogma of papal infallibility, which the Vatican Council defined as follows: "The Roman Pontiff, when he speaks *ex cathedra*, that is, when in discharge of the office of Pastor and Teacher of all Christians, by virtue of his supreme Apostolic authority he defines a doctrine regarding faith or morals to be held by the Universal Church, by the divine assistance promised to him in blessed Peter, is possessed of that infallibility with which the divine Redeemer willed that His Church should be endowed for defining doctrine regarding faith or morals: and that therefore such definitions of the Roman Pontiff are irreformable of themselves, and not from the consent of the Church."

The Church's Sanctifying Work

There has never been a time when the Church has not renewed upon her altars the redeeming Sacrifice of her Lord Jesus Christ and thus applied to the faithful the salvation which He established. At all times she has dispensed the sacraments to the faithful: baptism, confirmation, Holy Eucharist, penance, last anointing, holy orders, matrimony. Creatures useful to man have always been blessed and consecrated by the Church—field and bread, spring and dwelling, and now automobile and plane as well. The creative force of Christian life, nourished by the altar, has ever left its stamp upon any area in which Christian peoples have settled.

The Human Element in the Church

Nor, we must admit, has there ever been a time in the life of the Church when she did not also show the effects of the human element in her. This will be so until our Lord comes at the Last Judgment. Indeed He predicted it Himself, in His parables, which show how human weakness and malice do their work in the midst of the Church. He also predicted the rise of false prophets and false teachings. There have always been, and always will be, weeds among the wheat, chaff mixed with the grain; but the Christian does not let this confuse him. He knows that in the future as well as in the past these things are possible: unworthy popes, unworthy bishops and priests, an unworthy body of Catholics undeserving of the name of Christian. But all this does not threaten, let alone destroy, the holiness of the Church, in which "the Holy One of God" (Mark 1:24) continues to dwell. At the same time, our Lord's warning still stands: "It must needs be that such hurt should come, but woe to the man through whom it comes!" (Matthew 18:7).

Persecution and Oppression

We think of the Roman empire and the first centuries of the Church as "the time of martyrs." But the fact is that the Church has always suffered persecution. The time of martyrs is always with us. God does not wish to protect His Church from oppression by continually intervening in the history of the world. Yet it is precisely at times of utter distress that God grants the Church an increase of inner strength. Christ said, "Do not forget what I said to you, No servant can be greater than his master. They will persecute you just as they have persecuted me" (John 15:20). By persecution the Church is made like to her Lord; and she will follow Him in His glory also. "We must share his sufferings, if we are to share his glory. Not that I count these present sufferings as the measure of that glory which is to be revealed in us" (Romans 8:17-18).

The Powers of Darkness

The Church does constant battle against human weakness, blindness, and wickedness; but this is not all. She faces the hostile array of the powers of darkness—Satan and his angels. Our own times seem to find this particularly difficult to accept, as they ignore this part of fundamental reality. But whoever has followed the history of the Church closely and looked into it deeply, will have noticed a mysterious power constantly opposing God, difficult to grasp in its separate manifestations, but none the less definitely there—the prince of this world. The Church, however, has the promise of her Lord that the "gates of hell" will not prevail against her. "You must wear," says St. Paul, "all the weapons in God's armory, if you would find strength to resist the cunning of the devil. It is not against flesh and blood that we enter the lists; we have to do with princedoms and powers, with those who have mastery of the world in these dark days, with malign influences in an order higher than ours" (Ephesians 6:11,12).

"I Am With You All Days" (Matthew 28:20)

Neither human wickedness nor persecution nor the powers of darkness have been able to destroy the Church. The dark side of Church history thus becomes proof of God's unfailing assistance. Christ is with the Church "all days, even to the consummation of the world"; in addition to which, the Holy Spirit is the soul of the Church. This is a mystery. But we get some idea of the divine assistance when we consider that God at no time has failed to give the Church its saints—holy men and holy women whom the Holy Spirit made effective. When the capital city of the Roman empire needed to be won for Christ, St. Paul was called to do it. God has called countless others to holiness of life and utter devotion to a sublime task. Some of them witnessed to Christ by laying down their lives, others simply by performing the tasks of their ordinary lives. Whatever their occupation, their lives were holy, and their deeds helped to gain victories for the Church. The lives and works of the saints are the counterbalance to all the failings, weakness, and wickedness, which they outshine with their brilliance.

The Expectation of Our Lord's Second Coming

Because Jesus Christ overcame death by His Sacrifice on the Cross and won salvation for all men, every Christian awaits the final victory of the Kingdom of God. According to His promise and prophecy, all who believe in Him will share eternal life with all the angels and saints. The Christian is not ignorant of the battles and sufferings which will come before this final victory. He is not so superficial as to suppose that, in order to fulfill Christ's prophecies, the Church, preaching God's Kingdom and Christ's Holy Name throughout the whole world, will march on unopposed from victory to victory, from the conversion of one people to that of another. What the Christian does know with permanent and unshakable certitude is that the Church will win in the end. He looks ahead to the Second Coming of Christ, coming in glory to judge this world; and he says, in the words of St. John (Apocalypse 22:20), "Be it so, then; come, Lord Jesus!"

INDEX

INDEX